GLOBAL WARMING

AND THE CREATOR'S PLAN

GLOBAL
WARMING

AND THE CREATOR'S PLAN

Jay A. Auxt and Dr. William M. Curtis III

First printing: February 2009

ISBN-13: 978-0-89051-551-8
ISBN-10: 0-89051-551-4
Library of Congress Number: 2008943698

Cover Design by Nathan Pyles, Thinkpen Design, Inc.

Unless otherwise noted, all Scripture is from the King James Version of the Bible.

Printed in the United States of America

Please visit our website for other great titles:
www.masterbooks.net

For information regarding author interviews,
please contact the publicity department at (870) 438-5288.

Master
Books®
A Division of New Leaf Publishing Group

Contents

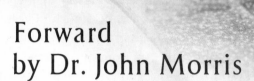

Forward
by Dr. John Morris

Global Warming has become the cause célèbre on the high school and university campus. It's even transformed into a major emphasis in elementary school classrooms. Students, with a grand desire for meaning, and to "slay the dragon" and "rescue the maiden" have latched onto it, fueling the movement and providing its ranks with millions of willing volunteers. They will gladly walk the street to spy on your "carbon footprint", and report all violators to the authorities. Teachers assign projects which further the goals, further cementing the conviction. An army is on the march, ablaze with a passion to do something meaningful, willing to do all within their power to protect the planet from overheating.

Scientists are not so sure. It may have been censored from your ears, but many knowledgeable experts have their reasons for dissent. Recently I spoke on "Creation and Current Issues" in a city housing a major government research lab. I am no expert on this issue, but it was one of the several briefly discussed. I showed only a few graphs documenting fluctuating world wide temperature trends and expressed my conviction that we have been shielded from much evidence in an apparent effort to manipulate social and political thought. Immediately, I was surrounded by numerous scientists, charging that I had not gone far enough, and encouraging me to continue challenging the global warming claim, for they are restricted from speaking out. Over the next few days, they showered me with more material than I could handle. Evidently there's another side to the issue.

Back in the mid seventies, I was heavily involved in the search for the remains of Noah's Ark, and had made contact with a highly placed official at the CIA, the Central Intelligence Agency. I had not realized it, but they gather intelligence of all sorts which might be of use in governmental decisions. Thus they are a major repository of weather data and global trends. The Institute for Creation Research, my sponsoring organization, had concluded the ice cap on Mount Ararat normally hides the Ark from view, but the Ark is probably exposed on warm, dry years, and I requested their aerial photography of the mountain from the years in question. Once they saw my voluminous evidence which showed, among other things, that in each year of the past century of minimal snow fall and elevated temperatures the Ark had been seen, they were most interested. I was left in the conference room while they studied their photos and files. They reemerged with discouraging news. Not only did they have no aerial surveillance which they could let me have, (the rest was "top secret") but they felt the search was futile at the present time. Not because it wasn't there, but because the earth was headed in to a prolonged cooling period. In fact, unless government stepped in to ward it off, we were entering a new Ice Age. Global cooling instead of global warming! Seems there is another side indeed.

This book presents that other side. No, it presents both sides, and analyzes the data objectively, without an overriding political agenda. More than that, it places global trends in a Biblical context, leaning on the perspective of the Creator of the weather to better understand the weather. Sounds reasonable. If we must develop a bias, we might as well adopt a proper bias, gleaning all the relevant information, and considered from a more complete perspective. This book also delves into human behavior as it relates to the one-sided claims, based on the thoughts of the Creator of humans, and His explanation of their behavior.

The Creator's evaluation can be summarized as the sudden appearance of all things, the earth, man and beast, all initially "very good" (Genesis 1:31). Man was given stewardship over God's creation, but soon, this perfect state was ruined by man's disobedience to God's plan, resulting in a downward spiraling of every system from perfection to its current state. The great Flood of Noah's day followed, which restructured the planet and forced all systems, including climate systems, to seek a new equilibrium. We live today in a fallen, flooded remnant of an original idyllic creation.

But the Creator's plan for Earth is not over. It has been delayed but not thwarted. We are told of coming climatic catastrophes culminating in a new earth, with the original perfection restored. Are we now seeing precursors? To top it off, we are promised a part in this New Earth which will last forever. In this timely new book, Jay Auxt and William Curtis III present what you need to know to understand current trends and future solutions.

Acknowledgements

The authors would like to express their most sincere appreciation to their wives and families for their loving support. Without their encouragement and support, this book would have never been possible. Also, praise the Lord! He has a plan, an eternal plan! The God of my rock; in him will I trust...: 2 Sam. 22:3

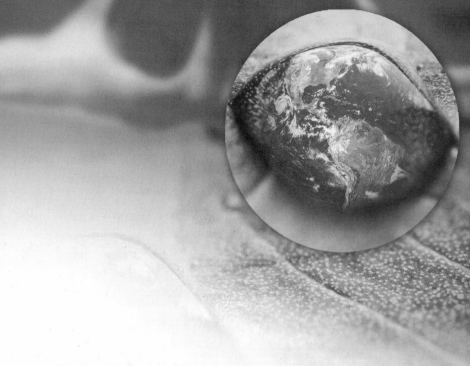

Introduction

How does "global warming" fit into "the Creator's plan"? Are these subjects even related? Does one's view of the earth, and specifically global warming, affect the Creator's plan for that person? Do one's actions affect the Creator's plan for this earth? Is global warming real? As a Christian steward of God's provision, what is my responsibility? These are just a few of the questions addressed in this book.

Any global view of the Creator's plan must consider what the Creator has revealed concerning His past, present, and future plans. The concept of global warming as an increasing threat to life here on earth leads us to an eschatological — or last days — scenario. The most definitive revelation regarding the last days of earth as we know it is given in God's revelation, the Bible.

This book will attempt to put global warming and the issues mentioned above into a historical, scientific, and biblical worldview by answering the following questions:

What is the history of this earth, including its environmental and geological conditions?

Is global warming happening, and if so, how long has it been going on?

Is it being exacerbated by man's activities in the 21st century?

Can man do anything to delay or reverse the effects of global warming?

How will this global warming affect our environment in the future?

Should the United States of America attempt to control global warming? If so, what methods should be used?

What is God's plan for you on this earth?

Global warming should not be seen as a predominately recent phenomenon. From the beginning of time, we see a constantly changing environment. The global Flood and Ice Age are prominent examples of extreme scenarios. Species such as the dinosaurs have gone extinct, and there is little mankind can do to alter this fact. The scientific and biblical aspects both come together in a cogent approach to what we should expect in this age, in turn directing and defining our actions both in the personal and political arena. God's original mandate included mankind's dominion and care for this world (see Gen. 1:28). However, sin's entrance into the world led to a geophysical and geopolitical war zone that continues to rage. The biblical/historical record of the earth's various environmental/geological configurations will be presented in depth with global warming in context.

God never intended for this present world configuration to last forever. The world was created to produce a family of God that would live and reign in the cosmos with God in a new earth (Rev. 21:1) for all eternity. As we know, this family is a free-willed species called humans, created in the image of God (see Gen. 1:26–27). Throughout history there have been specific stages in this creation of the family that involved both changing world scenarios and a redemptive program. This redemption plan presented to mankind a peek at the attributes of our Creator. Furthermore, it demanded the choice of God's person and will for our lives.

With both scientific and biblical facts this text will explore the past, present, and future world situation with the intent to understand what God would have us do in this present era. In addition, the biblical scenario for the last days and the future world will be presented to give hope in a dark day. God no more gives up on the earth than He gives up on us. He is no more finished with the earth than He is finished with us. God has promised to reverse the Curse on mankind and the physical earth to give us a new earth (John 14:1–4; Rev. 21:1).

But scientific and biblical facts are merely a distraction if not applied properly. Distractions can be devastating. So before we begin to examine the details of the Scriptures and science, let's review a famous event that is familiar to us all.

Date: approximately 1060 B.C.
Place: Shochoh (a city in Judah)
Cast of characters: A small young man and a very large warrior

The two characters are standing in the middle of a valley. Thousands of soldiers, fraught with anticipation, are standing on the hillsides waiting to see what will happen next. The very large warrior attempts to distract the small young man by intimidation. "Am I a dog, that thou comest to me with staves?" And he curses the young man by his gods. The large man attempts to distract the young man once again. "Come to me, and I will give thy flesh unto the fowls of the air, and to the beasts of the field." The small young man quietly opens his sling and places a small round stone in it. But it isn't just any sling or any stone. He has handcrafted the sling from the finest leather with the greatest perfection right to the minutest detail. The stone is carefully selected to be just the right size, the right shape, and the right texture to be flung from the sling with perfect accuracy. The small young man knows exactly what he is doing. He has confidently used this very sling to slay mighty lions and bears in the past. With that, the very large warrior raises his spear, a mighty spear. The head alone weighs 15 pounds! The rays of the sun glisten on the sharpened edge, suddenly causing the small young man to be distracted and fearful. The small young man slings the stone at the very large warrior, but he misses the mark. The rest is history.

Is that the way you remember the story? (See 1 Sam. 17:43–44.) With such a giant before him, did David have cause to be distracted and become afraid? Was he distracted? If he had been, the next scene would not have been very pretty for David. Even though he was highly skillful, his sling was carefully handcrafted, and his stones were meticulously selected, David's plans would have ended abruptly. But God's plans are never thwarted! The purpose of this book is not to puff you up (1 Cor. 4:6) with biblical or scientific knowledge and trivia facts, but to strengthen your walk with Christ, to gain confidence in His Word so that you will not be distracted by the master of deceit (Rev. 12:9), and ultimately that you may finish your course with joy, and the ministry, which you have received of the Lord Jesus, to testify the gospel of the grace of God, as did the writer of Acts (Acts 20:24). As a side benefit, you will also find this book to be a valuable resource when evaluating personal decisions such as purchases, voting, or vacations that may have spiritual or environmental consequences.

Chapter 1

A Biblical Basis

There went up a mist from the earth, and watered the whole face of the ground. . . . And a river went out of Eden to water the garden; and from thence it was parted, and became into four heads (Gen. 2:6,10).

Any text that attempts to combine history, science, and the biblical record should properly begin with the historical and scientific arguments for the veracity of the biblical record. Therefore, from a scientific and historical base we will begin there. Dr. Curtis's previous book, *The Last Days of the Longest War,*[1] gives both exegetical and scientific argument for a literal historical six-day creation. This book is centered on plans for you and the

---

1. William M. Curtis, *The Last Days of the Longest War* (Enumclaw, WA: WinePress Pub., 2005).

earth, especially as it relates to the so-called global warming crisis. Thus, we will argue for a biblical understanding of God's revelation regarding the earth — past, present, and future.

One need not be a scientist to understand that the earth is a young planet, having a cool, solid crust; it has a non-destructive, life-supporting atmosphere but is also made up of a molten core (see Gen. 1; Ps. 33:6–10). This young earth is ideally suited for 6,000 years of human habitation, but absolutely unable to exist for six billion years and be in its present state. Numerous scientists regularly present evidence that supports a biblically based creation. The International Conference on Creationism (ICC) hosts hundreds of scientists with peer-reviewed technical papers to present. The *Creation Research Society Quarterly* (CRSQ) publishes even more peer-reviewed papers every quarter. Scientific evidence to support the biblical account of creation abounds. Just to cite a few in this manuscript, we have selected the following:[2]

Phenomenon	Comment	Significance
Age of the universe	God tells us in His Word (Luke 3:23-38) how long a period it was from creation to Christ.	Evolution, on the other hand, *requires* billions of years, yet most data indicates that the earth is very young.
The earth's molten core	If the earth was billions of years old, it should have cooled and solidified by now.	If it had, the magnetic field that protects us from cosmic rays would be gone, and we would be dead.
The magnetic field	The magnetic field is decaying.	The measured decay rate does not fit an earth of billions of years.

---

2. D. Russell Humphreys, *Starlight & Time* (Green Forest, AR: Master Books, 1994); Don DeYoung, *Thousands . . . Not Billions* (Green Forest, AR: Master Books, 2005); John Morris and Steven A. Austin, *Footprints in the Ash* (Green Forest, AR: Master Books, 2003); Steven Austin, *Grand Canyon: Monument to Catastrophe* (Santee, CA: Institute for Creation Research, 1994); Duane Gish, *Evolution: The Fossils Still Say No!* (Santee, CA: Institute for Creation Research, 1996).

Phenomenon	Comment	Significance
Starlight	Dr. Russell Humphreys uses scripture (God "stretched out the heavens") and sound physics principles of general relativity to show how light from stars billions of light years away could be visible here on earth.	Starlight from distant stars is a serious stumbling block for many Christians. Dr. Humphreys' book *Starlight & Time* addresses this concern from a biblical and scientific approach.
Radioactive decay	The Institute for Creation Research spent $1.2M studying this subject. Evolutionary interpretation of this data severely contradicts itself.	Radioactive decay is also a serious stumbling block for many Christians. The book *Thousands . . . Not Billions* by Dr. DeYoung addresses this concern from a biblical and scientific approach.
Carbon–14 decay	This subset of radioactive decay strongly supports a young biblically based earth	Carbon dating of diamonds, which are impervious to contamination, indicates that the earth is very young.
Helium diffusion	Conventional radioactive decay methods suggest that zircons are billions of years old.	Helium diffusion data of the same zircon indicates that it is 6,000 years old (i.e., formed during the creation week).
Mount St. Helens	The Mount St. Helens eruption of May 18, 1980, shocked creation and evolutionary scientists by turning science completely upside-down in five different areas.	The book *Footprints in the Ash*, by Morris and Austin, shows how this single event illustrated how large scale sedimentation and erosion occurs very rapidly, supporting a biblical view of the Flood and creation.
The Grand Canyon	The Grand Canyon has always been considered a monument to millions of years of evolution.	The book *Grand Canyon: Monument to Catastrophe* by Dr. Steven Austin illustrates how the overwhelming evidence portrayed in the Grand Canyon clearly supports the concept of enormous floodwaters, not enormous numbers of years.

Phenomenon	Comment	Significance
Fossils	Evolutionists insist that the fossil record supports their theory.	*Evolution: The Fossils Still Say No!* by Dr. Duane Gish provides spectacular evidence that the fossil record fully supports the biblically based view of creation.
Recent ancient protein discoveries	Proteins deteriorate very quickly after death, yet recent dinosaurs have been discovered with proteins still intact.	These intact proteins support the concept of rapid deposition by a recent flood, not a slow death sixty million years ago.

The Bible tells us that the world was created very abruptly in six days only thousands of years ago. These are just a few of many topics of interest that support this biblically based view of our origins. Radioisotope decay is such a fascinating subject that a brief discussion is included in appendix 2. Evolutionists tend to worship *uniformitarianism*, the belief that *change* occurs very slowly at uniform rates. Appendix 5 of *The Defender's Study Bible*,[3] by Dr. Henry Morris, lists 68 uniformitarian methods of dating the earth that indicate that the earth cannot possibly be billions of years old. Scientific references are given for all 68 methods. Also, for a much more in-depth view of scientific data that supports a biblically based view, the recently published "Revised and Expanded" *The Young Earth*[4] by Dr. John Morris is a spectacular resource. In short, billions of years of the earth's existence do not stand up to the biblical testimony, the secular written history, or the scientific evidence.

We should not listen to the "politically correct" media that would like us to believe that all scientists support an evolutionary viewpoint. Dr. Jerry Bergman, Northwest State College, has accumulated a list of nearly 3,000 scientists who oppose this view

---

3. Henry M. Morris, *The Defender's Study Bible* (Grand Rapids, MI: World Publ., 1995).
4. John Morris, *The Young Earth* (Green Forest, AR: Master Books, 2007).

in favor of a more scientific view that supports a biblically based creation. Neither should we listen to the various positions of many Bible colleges, Christian colleges, and a vast list of churches and Christian ministries who try to allow for these positions of an old earth because they cannot handle science or the Scripture. If we fall for the evolutionary worldview of science based on "selective data" (and ignore considerable data that supports God's Word), we will almost certainly become prey for other "selective data" that misrepresents the global warming issue and possibly be distracted from God's precise plan for our life.

The biblical timeline begins with a recent creation of the heavens and the earth. This timeline is easily traced from the biblical records in Genesis and Luke as well as the secular historic record down to the present as we enter into the seventh millennium of our existence. Today we have many strong arguments for accepting this timeline from both history and science.

Like Basil and James Ussher did in their great literary works of the 4th and 16th centuries (respectively), we can deduce the earth's age by evaluating biblical and secular historical records side by side. The years from creation to the present may be added up from the data in Genesis and the rest of Scripture, and then correlated with secular historical records such as the laying of the cornerstone of Solomon's temple (see 1 Kings 6:1), bringing the timeline right up to today's calendar. We may determine the time of creation, the Genesis flood, Babel, the days the earth was divided into the present continents, the time of Abraham, the nation of Israel, the building of Solomon's temple, the Babylonian empire, the Medo/Persian empire, the days of Alexander the Great and the Macedonian/Greek or Hellenic empire, the Roman empire, the time of Jesus the Messiah 4,000 years after the creation (see Luke chapter 3), and the history of our world right down to today. For further study, some interesting notes on our current calendar are provided in appendix 1.

There are numerous ways of illustrating the biblical age of the earth. The following simple chart can be quickly and easily verified and is solid evidence that the earth is very young by any biblically based historical definition. In the following chart, the "age" column is the age of the "father" when the "son" is born. The "birth date" column is the age of the earth calculated by this biblical record.

Reference	Father	Age	Son	Birth Date
Gen. 2:19	Adam			0
Gen. 5:3	Adam	130	Seth	130
Gen. 5:6	Seth	105	Enos	235
Gen. 5:9	Enos	90	Cainan	325
Gen. 5:12	Cainan	70	Mahalaleel	395
Gen. 5:15	Mahalaleel	65	Jared	460
Gen. 5:18	Jared	162	Enoch	622
Gen. 5:21	Enoch	65	Methuselah	687
Gen. 5:25	Methuselah	187	Lamech	874
Gen. 5:28–29	Lamech	182	Noah	1056
Gen. 5:32	Noah	500	Shem, Ham, Japheth	1556
Gen. 11:10	Shem	100	Arphaxad	1656
Gen. 11:12	Arphaxad	35	Salah	1691
Gen. 11:14	Salah	30	Eber	1721
Gen. 11:16	Eber	34	Peleg	1755
Gen. 11:18	Peleg	30	Reu	1785
Gen. 11:20	Reu	32	Serug	1817
Gen. 11:22	Serug	30	Nahor	1847
Gen. 11:24	Nahor	29	Terah	1876
Gen. 11:26	Terah	70	Abram	1946
Gen. 21:3	Abram	100	Isaac	2046
Gen. 25:26	Isaac	60	Jacob	2106
Gen. 30	Jacob	Appr. 50	Joseph	2156
Gen. 37:2, 28	Joseph	17	Sent to Egypt	2173
Exod. 12:40	Jews in Egypt	430		2180 to 2610

This is an exercise that anyone can verify in a matter of a few minutes. For the sake of simplicity, let us assume that the Egyptian Empire, a well-established event, began around 3500 B.C. Many scholars believe that it began much later than that. If the Jews entered Egypt at the beginning of the empire, this would place the creation of the earth at 3500 + 2200 = 5700 B.C. at the very earliest! Many historical scholars believe the Jews entered Egypt around 1900 B.C., placing the creation around 4000 B.C. This is a key point in our discussion of global warming. If, on the other hand, humans have been on this planet for millions of years, the *supposed* current data for non-human-induced global warming (which we will discuss later in this chapter and in chapter 4) would indicate that the earth was much too cold for human habitation at the very time of their initial development.

Population

Population is an interesting subject in that it presents significant data to support the theory of a young earth and is also considered to be the major source for global warming. In this section, we touch on it as an evidence of a young, biblically based, earth.

The world population today relates to a growth from eight souls at the time of the flood, some 4,350 years ago. One of the key scientific/historical records to the veracity of Genesis is the human population of the earth, as is presented in depth in chapter 6, which agrees with the dates of the Genesis flood precisely, and no million-year evolution scenario can fit these data. There are historical records of a worldwide flood in practically every ethnic group around the world. There is no way to see millions of years in these data. Therefore, we may confidently approach the biblical record for an understanding of what God the Creator of earth has done and will do with His earth.

Biblical Authenticity

Although this is an extremely brief discussion of the biblical authenticity of the creation of the earth and mankind, it is crucial in the understanding of the global warming issue. Having established that the Bible is true, we can now develop an understanding of the principles of heat and global warming right from the very first day.

"In the beginning, God created the heaven and the earth. . . ."

We have heard that expression a million times. But let's examine this first day very closely since it is vital in understanding the nature of global warming. On the very first day of creation, God created mass, energy, time, and space as we currently understand them.[5]

- Verse 1: In creating "heaven" (in this case, "sky"), He created "space."

- Verse 1: In creating the "earth," He created "mass."

- Verse 3: In creating "light," He created "energy."

- Verse 5: "And the evening and the morning were the first day." Thus He also created "time."

This is generally considered to be quite obvious. But what may not be so obvious is that God braided these four entities together by the common laws of physics that He also created (see Col. 1:16) on the very same day. We can partially represent this interdependency by the following equations:

		Where:
Equation #1	$E=mc^l$	E = Energy
Equation #2	$D' = D\sqrt{1-\dfrac{v^2}{c^2}}$	M and m = Mass
Equation #3	$M' = \dfrac{M}{\sqrt{1-\dfrac{v^2}{c^2}}}$	D and D' = Distance
		T and T' = Time
Equation #4	$T' = \dfrac{T}{\sqrt{1-\dfrac{v^2}{c^2}}}$	c = The speed of light (distance divided by time)
		v = Velocity (distance divided by time)

5. Prior to the first day, there may very well have been some sort of "time" and "energy." God is eternal, with no beginning or end. Similarly, God Himself initially provided light (energy) prior to the creation of the sun and will do so again for the new earth (chapter 8). This concept of "time" and "energy" may be very different from what we currently understand. This question may be more of a philosophical question than one of science or Scripture and will not be addressed in this book.

Equation #1 is all that is necessary to tie energy, mass, distance, and time together. If equation #1 is a single strand of a cord, the other three equations make up other strands of this cord to form a rope that cannot be broken (refer to Eccles. 4:12).

These four entities — mass, energy, time, and space — are mathematically tied together and cannot be separated. God holds these laws *consistent* for us (see Col. 1:17). It is impossible to even imagine what the world would be like if these laws were not consistent from one day to the next. Fortunately, God has made a covenant with us to hold these laws constant (see Jer. 33:25–26). Consequently, we need to also recognize that all the laws of physics were also created on the very first day. (Since the evolutionary theories of the "big bang" and formation of the stars defies the first and second laws of thermodynamics, they seem to suggest that the laws of physics somehow also evolved over time, but we will not enter into that debate in this book.) The creation of all the laws of physics would naturally include these laws of thermodynamics. The second law of thermodynamics is an elusive one to clearly articulate, but in general terms, things naturally tend to go from order to disorder. We do not need to attempt to dissect all the different verbiage for the second law of thermodynamics to understand it within the context of global warming. We will demonstrate its applicability very simply with the following practical application:

> We can easily convert mechanical energy
> to heat energy with 100% efficiency, but we
> can never convert heat energy with 100%
> efficiency back into any other type of energy.

Thus we have now defined "entropy" and identified a source for global warming right from the very beginning of time! Adam and Eve were human beings. Their bodies had a metabolism. As such, their bodies burned carbohydrates, which in turn generated heat. This heat dissipated into the atmosphere in the form of "entropy" and can never be reused. The second law of thermodynamics was fully established right from the beginning of time. A source of heat for "global warming" is certainly a real phenomenon. It has existed since the first day of creation, but is it the phenomenon that is so widely propagated in the media today? Having a "source of heat" does not necessarily mean "warming" if other factors are involved.

One may raise the question then, "Does that mean that Adam and Eve were doomed to death right from the start?" No. "Wherefore, as by one man sin entered into the world, and death by sin; and so death passed upon all men, for that all have sinned" (Rom. 5:12). It is true that the second law of thermodynamics is responsible for the deterioration of our bodies today, but it is also true that our bodies are designed with the ability to regenerate and replace the building blocks of life; for example, to compensate for this law of physics. God declared the design of our bodies "good." Thus this "deterioration" was not "bad" but a natural function of life. It was not until after the Fall that our bodies could not fully compensate for this deterioration (see chapter 2).

With the authenticity of the Bible and the laws of physics confirmed from the beginning of time, we must also acknowledge, though, that the world has undergone several substantial changes. The geography described in the second chapter of Genesis corresponds to nothing in the present world configuration. Furthermore, this initial configuration was significantly changed at the Fall of man, as described in Genesis 3. The apostle Peter markedly points out in the third chapter of his second epistle that the Noachian flood destroyed the primeval world. Contrary to evolutionary uniformitarian ideology, the biblical record gives us three stages of geographical and meteorological change in the first 11 chapters of the Book of Genesis. These stages are:

- The initial configuration (Gen. 1 and 2)

- The pre-Flood conditions from the Fall of man to the global Flood (Gen. 3–7)

- The present geographical condition with its ever-decaying second law of thermodynamics configuration (Ps. 102:25–27; Isa. 51:6; Heb. 1:10–12)

It is with this understanding of God's working in His creation to bring about the plans and purpose for mankind and the new earth that He has promised (see 2 Pet. 3:16–19; Rev. 21 and 22) that "global warming" needs to be evaluated. Let us first attempt to define and describe the initial world configuration.

Chapter 2

Creation and the Initial World Configuration

For the LORD God had not caused it to rain upon the earth. . . . But there went up a mist from the earth, and watered the whole face of the ground (Gen. 2:5–6).

The late Dr. Henry Morris, in a footnote for Genesis 2:10 in his *Defender's Study Bible,* states that the geography described out of Eden in Genesis 2 "obviously corresponds to nothing in the present world."[1] The rivers described in Genesis 2 could not have derived their waters from rainfall, as Genesis 2:5 states that there was no rain on the earth in this configuration.

---

1. Morris, *The Defender's Study Bible.*

The Scripture defines the hydrological cycle before the Fall in Genesis 2:6 in this way: "There went up a mist from the earth, and watered the whole face of the ground." This watering of the ground collected into rivers, four of which are named in Genesis 2:10–14 as Pison, Gihon, Hiddekel, and Euphrates. This Euphrates should not be confused with the river today with the same name. The Genesis 2 Euphrates would have been utterly destroyed during the Flood.

This "mist from the earth" in the initial world configuration is vital as we consider the *initial climate* of the earth. Although archeologists have found no "weather reports" from this period of time, this mist suggests a very warm, tropical type of environment. In the Northern Hemisphere we often think of a mist as coming from a warm pavement on a steamy morning. However, this generally burns off as the day progresses. A more accurate depiction of this phenomenon may be that of a tropical rainforest with a very warm mist all day long. If there was no rainfall,

there must have been little to no wind. Also, according to Genesis 1:7, "God made the firmament, and divided the waters which were under the firmament from the waters which were above the firmament: and it was so." According to this passage, there was a canopy of water surrounding the earth. We know nothing about how much or how high this "canopy of water" was, so it is impossible to compare the amount of energy absorbed by the sun, reflected by the canopy, and produced by entropy. However, water reflects substantial sunlight and is a "greenhouse gas" that absorbs considerably more heat than carbon dioxide. Perhaps most importantly, we know that God said that this design was "good" and therefore, it was certainly in balance. (Conversely, a planet formed by random chance would certainly not be "good" and would likely be very unstable.) With no rain, little to no wind, and a canopy around the earth, we begin to get a picture of a fairly "greenhouse" warm environment for the entire earth. This is a key point. Although the second law of thermodynamics was generating heat in this "greenhouse" environment, the earth was declared "good" and therefore not getting any warmer.

With this limited hydrologic and geographic description of the initial world, the biological and botanical conditions should also be discussed.

Botanical Conditions

You have certainly heard the expression "It's a jungle out there," but have you ever actually been in a dense rainforest jungle? A dense rainforest jungle is almost difficult to imagine. The vegetation of a Northern Hemisphere forest pales compared to the vegetation of a dense rainforest. The visibility through the mist and vegetation of a rainforest is only a matter of a few yards. The initial world configuration was perfectly designed for a vegetarian world: "And God said, Behold, I have given you every herb bearing seed, which is upon the face of all the earth, and every tree, in which is the fruit of a tree yielding seed; to you it shall be for meat. And to every beast of the earth, and to every fowl of the air, and to every thing that creepeth upon the earth, wherein there is life, I have given every green herb for meat: and it was so" (Gen. 1:29–30). No animals were to be eaten. By design, this dense botanical state of the planet was ideal for the diet of man and animals.

Biological Conditions

There was no death in the initial world configuration (Gen. 2:17). It was not until sin entered the world that death entered the world (Rom. 5:12). Man had dominion (see Gen. 1:28), and everything was "very good" (see Gen. 1:31). Some people take issue with this passage since microbes and other tiny creeping creatures "die" in the normal process of another creature's life. For example, the human body is home to trillions of bacterial cells. Some of these bacterial cells are used to boost the immune system and are consequently killed in the process. However, the Bible always refers to "life" with respect to creatures with "blood" and "breath" (see Gen. 1:20, 6:17; Lev. 17:11). Microbes and other tiny creeping creatures have neither blood nor breath and therefore do not apply to this passage. These were the initial conditions prior to the Fall of mankind. This is an interesting point. The media would have us fear for our lives when it comes to the topic of global warming, yet the earth was likely much warmer than today at a time when death was nonexistent. Let's not draw any scientific or hermeneutical conclusions from this thought yet as we have numerous pages and thoughts to consider first.

Chapter 3

World Configuration from the Fall of Man to the Global Flood

Cursed is the ground for thy sake (Gen. 3:17).

This period of time includes two topics that, on the surface, may appear to be completely unrelated. However, they are both related to our discussion on "global warming and the Creator's plan."

The first is that of the subject of "authority." God is the author of authority (Gen. 3:16). Prior to the Fall, "authority" was a non-issue. Man walked sinless with God Himself. As a direct consequence of the Fall, and immediately following the Fall, God began to establish clear lines of authority. "Unto the woman he said, I will greatly multiply thy sorrow and thy conception; in sorrow thou shalt bring forth children; and thy desire shall be to thy husband, and he shall rule over thee" (Gen 3:16). Our Creator's plan includes clear lines of authority that are still established today (see Rom. 13:1; Eph. 6:1). As we continue through this book, we will see the ugly effects of godless authority and must continually remind ourselves that God uses sinners to accomplish His ultimate plan. Although we should never *justify* godless authority by this, we do need to remember that it was the godless Roman authorities that led Jesus Christ to His horrific death on the Cross, which in turn provided the stage for His Resurrection and the means for salvation for all believers!

Second, this period sets the stage for the Flood itself, which is certainly related to global warming and God's plan for us. From the initial creation described in Genesis chapters 1 and 2, there came an intervention into the world that had been created for mankind to dwell in and care for (see Gen. 1:28). This intervention was the appearance of the evil one to tempt mankind to disobey his Creator and attempt to become a god himself. This event described in Genesis 3 apparently happened shortly after mankind became aware of his environment, having explored his world and named the many creatures (Gen. 1–2), and was now exploring the idyllic garden in which he lived, called Eden (Gen. 2:8). With the appeal to disobey their Creator, Adam and Eve gave in to the temptation and caused the world to be condemned to a life of death and destruction, which abides to this day. Thus mankind, created with free will, was put into a system where there truly was a choice to follow the Creator or not. God will not have anyone in His family whom He has not chosen and who has not chosen Him. Thus, God manifests Himself as Creator and Redeemer, holy, almighty, and loving in Christ, the only true God. This is the whole theme of God's revelation recorded in the Bible, but the important aspect with respect to global warming and the Creator's plan in Genesis 3 is the changes to the world system with the Fall of man.

The Fall of mankind brought changes to biology, botany, geology, meteorology, and mankind's relation to one another. We will view these one at a time, presenting a brief description of these changes, with the existential evidence for the truth of the current system under the Curse given in Genesis 3:14–19.

> *And the LORD God said unto the serpent, Because thou hast done this, thou art cursed above all cattle, and above every beast of the field; upon thy belly shalt thou go, and dust shalt thou eat all the days of thy life: and I will put enmity between thee and the woman, and between thy seed and her seed; it shall bruise thy head, and thou shalt bruise his heel. Unto the woman he said, I will greatly multiply thy sorrow and thy conception; in sorrow thou shalt bring forth children; and thy desire [submission] shall be to thy husband, and he shall rule over thee. And unto Adam he said, Because thou hast hearkened unto the voice of thy wife, and hast eaten of the tree, of which I commanded thee, saying, Thou shalt not eat of it: cursed is the ground for thy sake; in sorrow shalt thou eat of it all the days of thy life; thorns also and thistles shall it bring forth to thee; and thou shalt eat the herb of the field; in the sweat of thy face shalt thou eat bread, till thou return unto the ground; for out of it wast thou taken; for dust thou art, and unto dust shalt thou return.*

Changes to Biology

As most people know, biology is the study of life. Life in mankind's current physical bodies was now to have an end (death), as mankind was declared to "return to dust" (v. 19). The truth of this event is revealed in the fact of universal death among the descendants of Adam. Romans 5:12 states clearly that in Adam all die. The regeneration of the building blocks of life was no longer sufficient to totally offset the natural deterioration due to the second law of thermodynamics as discussed in chapter 1. Not only were humans to die, but also the animal world was changed. The serpent was to be in the domain of Satan, and all animals were cursed (v. 14) and subject to death, which probably ushered in the carnivorous nature of many. It is interesting to note that in 1990 there lived in Australia a lion who was a complete vegetarian. Thus it could be assumed that these animals were not created with killing habits. The eating of animals is not mentioned in Scripture until after the Flood (see Gen. 9:3). Furthermore, the woman's pain and sorrow of conception and birth (v. 16) was not originally the case, and her subjection to the man would be greater because she was not obedient to her Creator.

Changes in Botany

The ground was cursed botanically, as it became hard work now to obtain food from it (v. 17). Thorns and thistles now permeate the environment (v. 18), vegetation now dies a natural death, and everything becomes harder for man (v. 19). It is interesting to note that, as Bible-believing Christians, we have a clear understanding as to why man does not live forever, but an evolutionist scratches his head as to why "death" would have ever evolved in the first place! (Many single-celled creatures do not die a "natural death." They replicate or may be killed by outside forces, but they have no natural death.) The second law of thermodynamics that states that everything is going downhill now also applies to life itself. This should compel all mankind to earnestly seek the Creator's plan as the only solution to this dilemma.

Changes in Geology

The earth/ground is also cursed (v. 17), and this leads to both environmental and geological challenges that increase with time. The dangers that we see every day in the form of volcanoes, tsunamis, and earthquakes are a result of these changes. How much this contributed to global warming during this time period no one will ever know, but scientists have calculated that volcanoes currently emit between 150 and 250 million tons of the greenhouse gas CO_2, into the atmosphere every year.

Changes in Meteorology

Genesis 2:6–14 indicates that there was no rain in the pre-cursed/initial environment. Much study has been performed regarding a high altitude canopy during the pre-Flood era. As discussed in chapter 2, this canopy could account for the worldwide vegetation apparent in the fossil record in what are today deserts and ice-covered areas. It could also account for the biblical long life span of mankind. Our purpose is not to deal with these issues. However, this Curse extends to meteorology as well as lightning and rain and can be considered one of the contributors to the Genesis Flood. This Curse continues to endanger life and limb for all of the earth's inhabitants until God creates the new earth as promised in Revelation 21 and 22.

The global Flood ended this environment approximately 2400 B.C. Much was said in the previous chapter about the evidence for this event to justify a literal historical reading of Genesis. It should be noted here, though, that some of the reason for the judgment of the world and all that is in it was that God did not choose to save all of His creation. Over 99 percent of the biosphere (living organisms) perished. Much of this ancient dead biosphere exists today in the form of *fossil fuels* — buried oil, natural gas, and coal. As we use these fossil fuels, we reintroduce them into the biosphere in the form of carbon dioxide.

Chapter 4

Present World Configuration and Global Warming

And ye shall hear of wars and rumours of wars: see that ye be not troubled: for all these things must come to pass, but the end is not yet (Matt. 24:6).

The passage from Matthew above is taken out of context, but we need to understand that this debate over global warming is becoming a fierce debate, if not "war." It is fought primarily by rumors. To obtain a full understanding of this topic, we must first lay down our weapons of rumors and pick up our swords of truth.

As you will recall, our two characters are standing in the middle of a valley. Thousands of soldiers, fraught with anticipation, are standing on the hillsides waiting to see what will happen next. The small young man looks at the very large warrior. He notices his helmet of brass, his coat of mail that must have weighed 125 pounds, the brass on his legs, and the "target" between his shoulders. *This fellow must be 10 feet tall*, the small young man thinks. *Has he really torn people apart, limb by limb, and fed them to the fowl of the air and the beasts of the field? Has this warrior really defeated whole armies single-handedly? Do swords and spears really bounce right off of his armor?* All of the past rumors suddenly paralyze the small young man. He now feels very awkward. "What am I doing here?" he asks. He tries to put one stone after another into his skillfully handcrafted sling, but one by one, he clumsily drops them on the ground.

Do we size up situations based on rumors? Do we become paralyzed by fear? Or do we consider our God-given duties and confidently do what is right in the sight of our Lord?

Christian Stewardship

As good stewards, Christians have an obligation to care for God's provisions for us (see Gen. 1:28; Matt. 25:14–30). This would be a natural extension of our gratefulness for all that He has so generously given to us. Genesis 1:28 is particularly interesting not only because of what it says, but because of what it does *not* say. Notice that according to this passage, we are not responsible for rain, wind, volcanoes, earthquakes, etc. These are left up to God. As Mark Twain once said, "Everyone complains about the weather, but no one does anything about it." God has only given us dominion over the things of this world where He has also given us some element of control. In like manner, we have virtually no control over the temperature of the world. Yet we constantly hear, "Man is responsible for global warming." As God's stewards, should we succumb to this rumor?

Noah's Flood

Talk about severe weather patterns! It rained for 40 days and 40 nights (Gen. 7:4), and the waters covered the highest mountains by 15 cubits (Gen. 7:20), enough for the keel of the ark to clear, and covered the earth for an entire year (Gen. 7:11, 8:13). The world had never seen weather of this sort prior to that event, and God has promised that we will never see weather like this again (Gen. 9:11). This single event has left evidence all over the world in the form of sedimentary rock, coal, oil, natural gas, petrified wood, caves, fossils, and the list goes on. After the Flood, the atmosphere would never be the same.

The Ice Age

The fountains of the great deep (Gen. 7:11) would have warmed the ocean waters for years to come. This warm ocean water (not cold atmospheric temperatures) would cause enormous precipitation. Winter precipitation comes in the form of snow — more snow than what would melt in the summer. As the snow accumulated year after year, glaciers began to form, and the Ice Age was born. The Book of Job was written very soon after the Flood. Job is enamored by snow and mentions it five different times. Living in the Middle East, it is easy to understand why he would be enamored. These references, along with others in the Book of Job that refer to other geological events of the Flood, suggest that these references to snow are references to the Ice Age.

Weather

"He causeth the vapours to ascend from the ends of the earth; he maketh lightnings for the rain; he bringeth the wind out of his treasuries" (Ps. 135:7). As discussed earlier, prior to the Flood, there was no rain on the earth. A continual mist watered the earth. After the Flood, this mist was gone. The earth now required rain for watering crops. Two great droughts stand out in the Old Testament.

The first was during the time of Joseph (Gen. 41:53–57). It was this drought that sent the Israelites to Egypt in hopes of purchasing grain (Gen. 42:1–3). You know the rest of the story. God used this event to set the stage for a mighty nation, the ten plagues, the Passover, and the first theocracy with Moses as their leader and penman of the Pentateuch.

The second great drought was during the time of Elijah. Not only was there no rain, but there was also no dew (1 Kings 17:1). It was this drought that set the stage for the first resurrection recorded in the Bible, the resurrection of the widow's son (1 Kings 17:22).

God also uses weather to chasten those He loves (Heb. 12:6). One particular case that comes to mind is that of Jonah. Jonah was clearly sent to Nineveh but instead he chose to head in the opposite direction. But he could not hide from God. God used a great storm to bring Jonah back to Him. "So they took up Jonah, and cast him forth into the sea: and the sea ceased from her raging" (Jon. 1:15).

We serve a mighty God. Not only can He use weather for numerous reasons, but He can even alter the paths of celestial beings to serve His purpose. Let's look at Joshua 10:13: "And the sun stood still, and the moon stayed, until the people had avenged themselves upon their enemies. Is not this written in the book of Jasher? So the sun stood still in the midst of heaven, and hasted not to go down about a whole day."

Let's look first at the possible scientific explanations for this event. Did the sun actually stand still? Well, if it actually stopped its rotational orbit within the Milky Way, the earth would have been thrown out of the sun's orbit, so that cannot be an explanation. However, this is written from earth's perspective and not from the sun's. That means the earth's rotation must have stopped. But that is not possible either. The rotational surface speed of the earth is over 1,000 miles per hour. Yes, people standing on the earth are actually moving at over 1,000 miles per hour! We don't feel it because the air is moving with us. But imagine what would happen if someone slammed on the brakes at that speed!

Well, forget the sun for a moment. Maybe stopping the moon

will be easier to explain scientifically. For it to appear "stopped" it would have to actually revolve around the earth exactly once per day. Wow! That's quite a change! It currently takes over 27 days to circle the earth. If the moon sped up to that speed, it would certainly sling out of orbit and off into space! Maybe Joshua just made it all up. Well — that doesn't work either. This event is documented in other cultures such as Greece, Egypt, and even the Western Hemisphere. With all our knowledge about the solar system, we cannot even imagine an explanation for this event. Now that's quite a miracle, isn't it? In a word, YES! But then your very existence here on earth is no less of a miracle. You are part of the Creator's plan. God put you here with a purpose.

These are all Old Testament examples, but does God still control the weather? Absolutely. "And there arose a great storm of wind, and the waves beat into the ship, so that it was now full. And he was in the hinder part of the ship, asleep on a pillow: and they awake him, and say unto him, Master, carest thou not that we perish? And he arose, and rebuked the wind, and said unto the sea, Peace, be still. And the wind ceased, and there was a great calm. And he said unto them, Why are ye so fearful? how is it that ye have no faith?" (Mark 4:37–40).

It is also interesting to note that these events occurred rapidly or instantly. If God can control these incredible events and use them to serve His purpose, then clearly God can control slight temperature variations and use global warming to serve His purpose as well.

Media Sensationalism

With the bounty and majesty of all God's miracles, it is difficult to imagine why the world's media thrives on sensationalism. But that is the way the secular world operates. In the words of William Paley in his book *Natural Theology*, "One great cause of our insensibility to the goodness of the Creator is the very extensiveness of His bounty. . . . The common benefits of our nature entirely escape us. Yet these are *the great* things!"[1]

For the media industry, it's simply a matter of "competition." In order for one media to outsell the other, the news must be more sensational. This leads to excessive hype. A quick search on the Internet for the term "global warming" revealed over 56 million results! How are we to sort out which information is hype and which is valid? Consider the following report on climate change. Read it very carefully to make sure you absorb the full impact. "There are ominous signs that the earth's weather patterns have begun to change dramatically and that these changes may portend a drastic decline in food production — with serious political implications for just about every nation on earth. The drop in food output could begin quite soon, perhaps only ten years from now." Even if this claim is exaggerated, if partially true, it spells deep trouble possibly beginning in as little as ten years. Fortunately, it was pure hype — pure sensationalism. Yes, "was," as in "past tense." It was not referring to global warming. It was referring to the coming Ice Age as reported in the April 28, 1975, issue of *Newsweek*. The concerns were not completely unfounded. They were based on "selective data." For example, from 1955 through 1974, five all-time record low temperatures were set here in the United States.

Moving to the present, consider a more recent report (*MSNBC*, August 7, 2007) that claimed "a series of record-breaking events in 2007" including "flooding in Asia, heat waves in Europe, and snowfall in South Africa." The article continued: "severe monsoon floods across South Asia, abnormally heavy rains in northern Europe, China, Sudan, Mozambique, and Uruguay, extreme heat waves in southeastern Europe and Russia, and unusual snowfall in South Africa and South America." Has this hype succeeded in scaring you yet? There's more. "South Africa in June had its first significant snowfall since 1981. . . . In South America, Uruguay in May had its worst flooding since 1959 . . . Buenos Aires saw snow in July for the first time since 1918." Or did those figures shock

---

1. William Paley, *Natural Theology* (Oxford: Oxford University Press, 2006).

you? The truth is, we should be seeing record-breaking years every year. The world is huge and the weather is diverse. There will be hot spots, cold spots, wet spots, and dry spots every year. As you examine the statements above, it can be determined that:

• South Africa had a more significant snowfall in 1981;

• Uruguay had worse flooding in 1959; and

• Buenos Aires saw more snow in 1918.

So much for the hype. Looking at it from that perspective, it sounds like the weather is actually improving. This article is not alone. This is just one of many reports every single day. It is strictly hype. We keep hearing about "warmest since _____." But for global warming to truly be real, we should be regularly hearing reports of "warmest ever ____." We should also not be hearing "Coldest ever in the Midwest," like we heard in the winter of 2008. How does "The coldest ever in the Midwest" fit into global warming? In January of 2009 Alaska was also having "coldest ever" records. Temperatures dropped to 60 below and stayed there for two weeks! This record cold snap was regularly referred to as *an extreme event*. However, Alaska was not unique! According to MSNBC.com, on January 16th, 2009 thirteen states were having subzero temperatures:

-50 in Big Black River, MA
-46 in Embarrass, MN
-42 in Island Pond, VT
-42 in Necedah, WI
-39 in Berlin, NH
-38 in Monticello, IA
-36 in Sterling, IL
-35 in Paradox, NY
-26 in Stambaugh, MI
-20 in Valparaiso, IN

-19 in Lawton, PA

-16 in Snowshoe Mountain, WV

-14 in Dayton, OH

A couple of these individual temperatures may have set new record lows. For this cold to span so many states in a single day must shatter many records. But that doesn't put a stop to all the hype. Unfortunately, Joseph Goebbels (Nazi propagandist) was right about one thing. He said, "If you tell a lie big enough and keep repeating it, people will eventually come to believe it." Far too many people believe this "hype" about man-made global warming.

But we are not just hearing about temperature changes. We are hearing about the state of Florida almost completely disappearing due to rising oceans. We hear about hurricanes so vicious that they threaten to destroy our entire coastline and hundreds of miles inland. We are told that runaway warming will turn vast farmland into deserts. As a result, we will suffer from widespread famine and the spread of worldwide diseases like the earth has never seen before. We hear projected dates as early as 2010 (well, that one is getting fairly close now), 2050, and 2100 as particular doomsdays. We hear about mass extinction of plants and animals. Is the sky really falling?

Plant and Animal Extinction

"Human beings are currently causing the greatest mass extinction of species since the extinction of the dinosaurs 65 million years ago. If present trends continue, one half of all species of life on earth will be extinct in less than 100 years, as a result of habitat destruction, pollution, invasive species, and climate change."[2] As you scroll down the Web site where this statement is made, you will find over 400 links to articles indicating that you are responsible for this massive kill.

We have been hearing this accusation for decades, and the battle cries are rapidly increasing. We could examine countless examples. Let's look at just a few.

---

2. http://www.well.com/~davidu/extinction.html.

Hurricane Katrina killed over 1,800 people and caused over $80 billion of damage. We are told that Hurricane Katrina was so devastating because of your contribution toward global warming. You are expected to believe that you are to blame, not the storm, for this death and destruction. Furthermore, ever since Hurricane Katrina struck New Orleans on August 29, 2005, we keep hearing of plants and animals threatened in the New Orleans wetlands and bayous due to the rising sea level due to global warming. This is another outrageous (but effective) form of media hype. The truth is, areas of New Orleans are rapidly sinking at a rate of a quarter inch to over one inch per year (*Science Daily*, June 1, 2006). This is known as "subsidence", which is mostly man-induced but has nothing to do with global warming. Subsidence is caused by numerous factors, but in New Orleans it is primarily caused by the pumping of water out from under the city. New Orleans, being below sea level, must continually pump the groundwater out from under the city or there would be "artesian spring water" surfacing everywhere. The combination of this pumping and the weight of the buildings causes the land to continually subside. Some of the levees protecting New Orleans have subsided three feet. Most of the flooding was not caused by the storm waters topping the levees. Differential settlement (settling at different rates) of a levee due to this subsidence places additional "bending stresses" on the levee and is believed to have been one of the major causes of levee failures. It was the additional stress of this differential settlement in conjunction with the weight of the water that caused the failures. Not global warming.

The purpose of levees is also often misunderstood. It is widely believed that the purpose of levees is to "prevent" flooding. This is not the case. A system of levees serves to *relocate* flood waters from one location to an alternate location. Hopefully the flood waters will do less damage at these "alternate locations." However, levees also raise the elevation of flood waters. As we continue to build in low-lying areas, land that was once considered "safe" becomes a major target for flooding.

Also included in this media hype and fear tactics, we constantly hear about the endangered species that will soon become extinct due to man's irresponsible global warming. Some are so well choreographed that we actually pay good money to subject ourselves to subtle but colossal propaganda. One such example is the movie *Arctic Tale*. This movie by Paramount and National Geographic is an extremely well-produced "arctic tale" of a mama bear and a baby bear with as much credibility as the old fairy tale of a mama bear, papa bear, and three little cubs. This 86-minute movie will steal your heart as it portrays the tragic life of a mama polar bear and her two poor polar bear cubs trying to survive abnormally warm weather. The melodrama unfolds with comments describing their difficulties as "changes never before encountered by their species," and turning these "rightful masters into refugees." It includes spectacular footage of a mama bear and two cubs perfectly happy in a harsh "normal" winter. It then shows more spectacular footage of a mild winter with considerably less arctic ice the very next year where life is intolerable and one little bear cub dies due to the warmth. What a bizarre suggestion! Global warming, a change of temperature of maybe half a degree over many decades, changed the entire habitat for polar bears in one year? There is no mention of the fact that ocean currents carry thousands of times more heating and cooling capacity than the air, yet we are expected to believe that this little cub died because we drove our car to work today and supplied electric power to our house from a fossil fuel plant. There is also no mention of the fact that the Arctic volcanoes have been extremely active in recent years! Yes, live volcanoes erupting on the Arctic Ocean floor! Yet, this ice melt is all portrayed as man's fault due to global warming, and if we do not act quickly, these cute little polar bears will soon become extinct. Truth be known, having been on the Arctic ice in the dead of winter on multiple occasions (a photo of our most luxurious "ice camp" is shown on the next page), let me assure you that survival in the Arctic is never easy. Animals succumb to the cold every year.

Arctic ice camp

The arctic certainly does not stand alone. The September 2004 edition of the *National Geographic Magazine* was dedicated to global warming (but certainly made no mention of "God's plan"). According to this article, the tropical Fleischmann's glass frog, a miniature translucent frog, "is barely hanging on" with "more than half of that region's frog species also declined or vanished." You wouldn't know it by researching this frog in Costa Rica on the Internet. According to the data, they are extremely abundant.

The same magazine shows a full-size, two-page photo of a few Adélie penguins with the caption, "This colony dwindled from 320 breeding pairs to 54 between 1990 and 2004." What they bury in the 75 pages of text is that the Adélie penguin is one of the most common and well-known penguins in Antarctica with 2.5 million pairs!

The article continues, "Four million acres of Alaska spruce . . . stand dead, victims of the spruce bark beetle. The warmth has boosted the numbers of mature

beetles." What they fail to tell you is that these four million acres have been dying for over 80 years and that only extremely cold, snowless winters will put these beetles back into check.

The *National Geographic* article continues with story after story of "partial information" of various plants and animals. We are now expected to believe that the endangerment of countless plant and animal species (even if they live many thousands of miles away from us) is our fault. As Christians, we certainly want to be good stewards of His provisions. So what is this so-called global warming, and should we really cry ourselves to sleep with personal guilt every night?

Man-made Global Warming

We constantly hear the term "global warming," but what is it? The term portrays an assumption that the temperature of the entire world (the *globe*) is actually increasing (getting *warmer*). The story is as follows:

1. Man burns fossil fuels (coal, oil, and gas) for energy.
2. This combustion produces carbon dioxide.
3. Carbon dioxide holds more heat than the other constituents of our atmosphere.
4. This excess heat causes the earth to get warmer.
5. This increase in temperature will cause:
   a. the melting of glaciers and Arctic and Antarctic ice;
   b. the sea level to rise, causing massive flooding;
   c. substantially stronger hurricanes;
   d. the destruction of many plants and animals;
   e. a complete imbalance of the world's ecosystem;
   f. and ultimately the destruction of the world as we know it.

As you can see, the phrase "global warming" has significant, scary ramifications. As is the case with any statement, if we hear it often enough, we tend to believe it is true, regardless of the merit. If you doubt this trend, consider the following statement and fill in the blank, "_____ tastes good, like a cigarette should." That statement was banned from radio and television commercials on February 5, 1969 (over 40 years ago), yet if is still familiar to many Americans even today. Advertising agencies spend millions of dollars to ensure that you hear the same message as often as possible to entice you to take action. The phrase "global warming" is not banned from radio and television broadcasts and is intended to entice you to certain actions as well. This "enticement" is not just at local or personal levels, for it has become a worldwide epidemic.

Intergovernmental Panel on Climate Change (IPCC)

Consider the following statement by the 2007 Intergovernmental Panel on Climate Change (IPCC):

> Continued greenhouse gas emissions at or above current rates would cause further warming and induce many changes in the global climate system during the 21st century that would *very likely* be larger than those observed during the 20th century. [Italics in the original text]

The purpose of this panel sponsored by the United Nations Environment Program (UNEP) and the World Meteorological Organization (WMO) is to provide guidelines to entice countries to take action in environmental policies. This is not just "opinion." It is clearly stated on the title page of their report:

> This Summary *for Policymakers* was formally approved at the 10th Session of Working Group I of the IPCC, Paris, February 2007 [italics mine].

But does this international policymaker statement actually reflect the "present world configuration" that we see today? Notice that the statement includes the phrase "further warming." This statement *assumes* that warming already exists. However, long-term temperature data is conspicuously absent from the report (and every global warming report) because long-term temperature data does not exist. Galileo invented the first thermometer (based on water density) in 1593, but temperature standardization was not even proposed until 1913 by the International Committee for Weights and Measures. It took another 55 years for the international community to arrive at a standard. That being the case, *every* single statement that you hear regarding long-term temperature increases is referring to significant *assumptions*. Not only does this temperature data not exist currently, but it is also impossible to obtain.

"There's no question that the Earth is getting hotter — and fast" (*National Geographic*, September 2004). If that is really true, the temperature data should be easy to verify. Let's see if that is, in fact, the case.

Temperature Measurements

It is amazing how many people believe they can actually "feel" this difference in temperature due to global warming. "Yep, this heat and drought just gets worse every year." Let's stop and think about that. We have not discussed the actual numbers yet, but can you really tell the difference between a one-degree temperature difference from one day to the next? Even if you could, do you think that the humidity and extent of cloud cover would present a greater "feeling" of temperature change than a single degree of actual change? Of course. So how could anyone possibly "feel" a single degree temperature change over the course of 50 years? This is utterly impossible. Yet, we almost all "feel" like it is warmer, because of the constant media hype discussed earlier. "But I 'remember' bigger snows and colder weather when I was a child," you might say. Yes. Our memory is like that. We tend to remember the extremes. With all the hype about global *warming*, we are much more likely to remember the cold weather extremes than warm weather extremes. That is the way our psychology works. Therefore, to determine if we actually are experiencing true "global warming" we need solid, convincing data.

Before continuing we need to also establish, "Who is required to provide this convincing data, this burden of proof?" It has often been stated that extraordinary claims require extraordinary evidence to support such claims. A common question is, "What is the proof that the earth is not warming?" Data will be provided later in this chapter that clearly does not support global warming, but the burden of proof for providing convincing data of global warming falls solely on those who perpetrate this "extraordinary claim."

There is an old proverb, "If you have one watch, you always know what time it is. If you have two, you never know." The same is true of temperature. "If you have one thermometer, you always know what the temperature is. If you have two, you never know."

As you can imagine, temperature has always been an elusive measurement. It was defined as the International Practical Temperature Scale in 1968 and was even redefined again as the International Temperature Scale in 1990. The International Practical Temperature Scale of 1968 is sometimes referred to as the "T1 scale," and the International Temperature Scale of 1990 as the "T2 scale." As a humorous anecdote, the next time someone starts talking to you about global warming, look at them inquisitively and ask, "Are you referring to temperature data measured on the T1 scale, or T2 scale?" Rest assured — that will be a conversation stopper. This will also give you the opportunity to point out that there is no temperature data to support global warming. This is not just a trivia question either. Although the difference between the T1 scale and the T2 scale is small, it would have an enormous effect on *apparent* global changes if assumed to be a real change of temperature and then extrapolated over a hundred years or so. Small errors extrapolated over long periods of time become enormous errors. An example of extrapolating small errors is as follows.

You have two laboratory grade mercury thermometers that

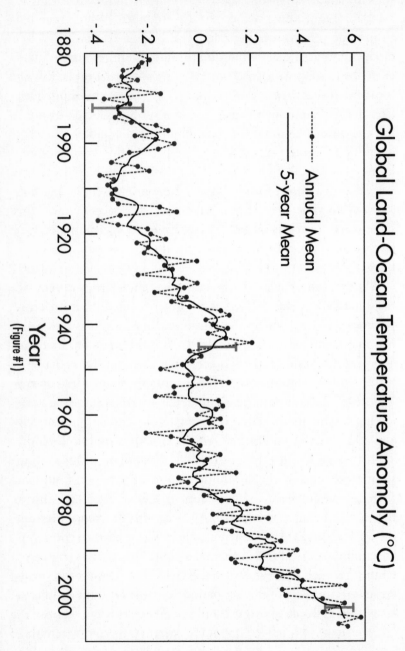

Global Land-Ocean Temperature Anomoly (°C)

Temperature Anomaly °C

Year
(Figure #1)

Annual Mean

5-year Mean

are both in the shade, one on the front porch, and one on the back porch. You notice that the one on the front porch reads 0.5 degrees higher than the one 50 feet away on the back porch. You want to go to town to pick up the mail and need to know how to dress. Town is nearly three miles away, which is about 15,000 feet. You extrapolate this 0.5-degree difference from the front of your house to the rear of the house, 50 feet apart, to town that is 15,000 feet away and come up with a downtown temperature of

$$\Delta T = 0.5 \times \frac{15{,}000}{50} = 150$$

Consequently, you can scientifically determine that it is 150 degrees warmer in town than at your house. Obviously this example is absurd, but it illustrates the significance of extrapolating minor errors. Extrapolating small errors due to temperature measurement variances over long periods of time suffers from the same effect.

This is not to suggest that temperature charts do not exist. Obviously they do. The chart (figure #1) should be from a reliable source. It came from a September 25, 2006, NASA Goddard Institute for Space Studies (GISS) report entitled "NASA Study Finds World Warmth Edging Ancient Levels." This chart looks quite detailed and complete — but where did the data come from, how it was obtained, how many locations were considered, how often were the temperatures recorded, and how were non-standard temperatures interpreted? This is not to suggest that the data was pulled out of the air or simply made up. This is also not to suggest that answers to these questions do not exist. The problem is that they are very difficult to find and verify. We are simply asked to accept it as fact. Also, note that the authors of this chart expect you to believe that the first 30 years of this global data (when no international standards on temperature existed) are just as credible as the most recent 30 years of data, the period of supposed concern. If the first 30 years of this data are obviously unreliable, why should we accept the most recent 30 years of data? It is not the intent to simply pick on NASA GISS. This is a typical example of

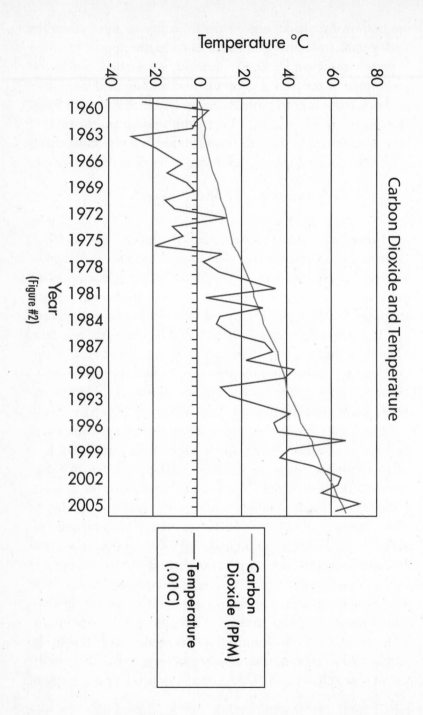

Temperature °C

Carbon Dioxide and Temperature

Year
(Figure #2)

Carbon
Dioxide (PPM)

Temperature
(.01C)

the baseless global warming *temperature* data. It is *baseless* because no true data, for even as little as 100 years, exists.

As discussed in chapter 2, the global warming crisis is based on "selective data." This selective data is then "extrapolated" into the future to predict our rapid demise. Interesting to note, they never extrapolate this data backward into the past! If we consider extrapolating global warming from 1960 to 2000 into the future to be valid, then we should naturally consider extrapolating into the past equally valid. So let's take the 1880 to 1940 data of 0.005 degrees per decade (from their chart above) back to man's supposed evolutionary origin of 250,000 years ago. (Global warming fears are highly dependent on evolutionary dogma. If they believe that it is valid to extrapolate into the distant future, we should also be able to extrapolate into the distant past. See the section on atmospheric stability later in this chapter.) By multiplying 0.005 degrees per decade times 25,000 decades, we can confidently state that the earth was 125 degrees colder back when man first evolved. Hopefully they had warm coats! Obviously — even though the math works — extrapolating selective data is fallacious pseudo–science. Evidently, there must be some other data that is fueling this global warming hysteria.

Carbon Dioxide Measurements

As the story goes, the more carbon dioxide there is in the atmosphere, the higher the global temperature. Carbon dioxide retains heat more so than the nitrogen and oxygen in the atmosphere. On the surface, this theory makes sense. In this next section, we will show that this "story" is over-simplified and that other data and aspects of carbon dioxide are being completely ignored.

But let's not avoid the subject of temperature altogether. We can look at recent temperature and carbon dioxide measurements and ask some reasonable questions. The temperature data on the chart (figure #2) came from NASA GISS. The carbon dioxide data came from the Mauna Loa Observatory. The baseline for this data is 1959, when the carbon dioxide level was 317 ppm and the average global temperature was 14 degrees Celsius. There-fore, the actual parts per million (ppm) of carbon dioxide on this chart would be plus 317 ppm, which was the value in 1959. For example, the atmospheric carbon dioxide level of 1992 would be "40 + 317," which equals "357 ppm." The temperature data has been multiplied by 100 in order to make the changes more rec-ognizable. Therefore, the actual temperature would be "the chart data divided by 100 plus 14 degrees Celsius." For example, the temperature in 1995 would be 41 divided by 100 plus 14, which equals 14.41 degrees Celsius.

At a glance, it certainly appears that increased carbon dioxide is causing global increases in temperature. But let's not be over-reactive by just a quick glance. From 1992 to 2003, the carbon dioxide level increased by 20 ppm, and the global temperature increased by 0.50 degrees. Yet from 1959 to 1978 the carbon dioxide level increased by the same amount (20 ppm) with virtu-ally no increase in global temperature. Also, from 1976 to 1981 the temperature soared by 0.54 degrees at a time when the carbon dioxide level increased by only 8 ppm. It certainly appears that there is no correlation between carbon dioxide concentrations and global temperature.

Furthermore, as you look at this graph you will notice that the carbon dioxide level never decreases. It has increased every year from 1959 until the present. Yet the global temperature fluctuates wildly during the same time period. We can attribute the 0.3 degree temperature drop from 1981 to 1982 to the enormous ash cloud caused by the eruption of Mount St. Helens that blocked signifi-cant sunlight for a year, but the other temperature dips (some of which are much larger than 0.3 degrees) are totally unexplainable by the "carbon dioxide — global warming" theory. Consequently, it can clearly be stated that global warming cannot be supported by the carbon dioxide data that is available. Obviously, other factors play a considerable role in the temperature of the earth.

The earth has gotten warmer over the past 50 years. But is this "global warming" (i.e., caused by man's carbon dioxide pollution) or is it merely a temporary swing or caused by something entirely unknown and uncontrolled by man?

The next chart (figure #3) shows temperatures just in the United States over the past century. This data comes from the National Climate Data Center (NCDC) of NOAA. At least it eliminates some of the variables due to non-standard temperature measurements (or unknown standards) in other countries around the globe. Analyzing the data from this chart, the rate of temperature increase over the first 50 years was four times greater than the rate of temperature increase the second 50 years. According to this data, the "warming" of the second half of the century is only one-fourth that of the first half. This temperature data actually indicates that warming has decreased during our increased production of greenhouse gasses.

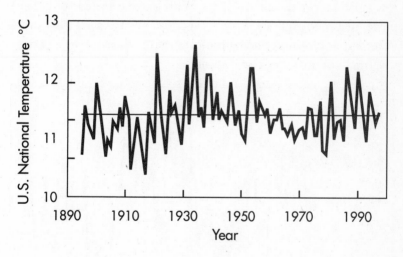

(Figure #3)

Before leaving our discussion on carbon dioxide, there is one more crucial point to make. As discussed in chapter 3, the carbon dioxide argument also totally disregards the fact that these so–called human-produced carbons were all a natural, active part of the biosphere prior to the Flood. This fact will always be completely disregarded by the proponents of global warming because of their evolutionary perspective. In their minds, a worldwide flood cannot possibly explain the worldwide flood deposits. That would be unthinkable. The carbon in the biosphere prior to Noah's flood dwarfs the current carbon of today. If the earth thrived on that massive carbon prior to the Flood, it can support it again. Naturally we cannot introduce all of this carbon back into the biosphere overnight, but we must agree that the natural forces of the earth (designed by God) will return this carbon back to a healthy equilibrium, or we must deny the conclusive scientific evidence that it was ever healthy in the first place.

Since looking at pinpoint temperature measurements around the earth does not support global warming, perhaps they need temperature measurements from larger geographical areas.

Additional Measurement Techniques

The data in the chart (figure #4) is based on single point surface measurements. In this next section, we will show that other temperature measurements indicate that the earth is not getting warmer and may even be cooling.

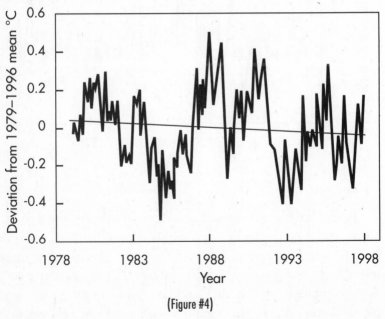

(Figure #4)

What if we used a satellite to measure large areas of temperature? The data was collected by the Satellite Microwave Sounding Unit (MSU) as published in *Science* (issue #247) and *Nature* (issue #389) magazines. According to this data, the earth's temperature has actually been *decreasing* since 1979. Shouldn't the data indicate increasing temperatures?

Which data is correct? The NASA GISS data, the NCDC data, or the MSU data? Clearly, scientists select the data that supports their cause.

As long as we are choosing data to consider, we should consider Mars and the Neptune moon, Triton. According to NASA Ames Research Laboratory, the temperature of Mars has "increased dramatically" (more than one degree Fahrenheit) over the past 30 years. Similarly, according to scientists at MIT, Lowell Observatory, and Williams College, the temperature on Triton increased three degrees in only ten years. Is that man's fault, as well? What does this temperature data really mean? Or does it mean anything at all?

Now that we have firmly established that *temperature data* to support global warming does not exist and cannot possibly exist, the following questions still remain unanswered: "Does human-produced global warming really exist in this present world configuration? If so, is it dangerous? And if so, is there anything we can do about it?"

The answer to the first question is very simple: we do not know. Without temperature data, how could we know? Proponents of global warming blame humanly produced carbon dioxide due to the burning of fossil fuels such as wood, coal, oil, and gas (the once-living biosphere that was buried during the great Flood) as the enemy. Since carbon dioxide holds more heat than the other constituents of our atmosphere, it is assumed that if man increases the carbon dioxide level, then the temperature must also increase. However, temperature data does not support this notion. According to the Earth System Research Laboratory, data taken from the Mauna Loa Observatory indicates that the average carbon dioxide

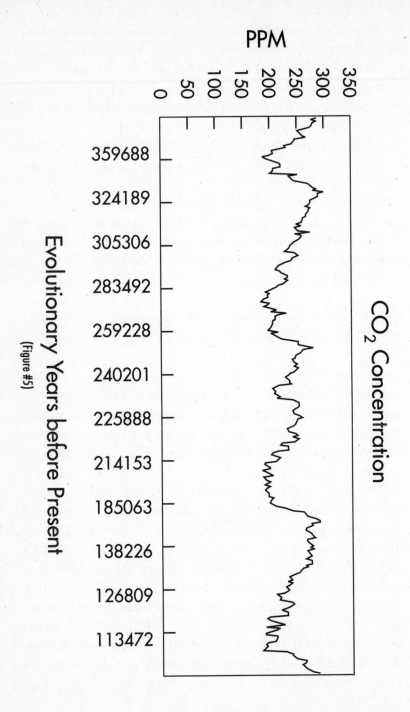

PPM

CO₂ Concentration

Evolutionary Years before Present

(Figure #5)

increase per year over the past 48 years has been 1.4 ppm. However, the increase in 1998 was more than double the average at 2.95 ppm. Did the world double its energy output (and carbon dioxide emissions) that year? Did this trigger exceptionally hot years to follow? Not in the least. According to the Goddard Institute for Space Studies (GISS) Surface Temperature Analysis, 1998 was un-usually warm, a few tenths of a degree warmer than the few years before or after 1998. If the increases in carbon dioxide in 1998 truly caused global warming, then the years following 1998 should remain warmer. They did not. Could it be that the exceptional carbon dioxide increase in 1998 was caused by a warmer than normal year? When the atmospheric temperature increases, carbon dioxide is released from oceans. Think about that. It is possible that the carbon dioxide level is increasing because of the temperature, not the other way around. We simply do not know.

Nevertheless, proponents of global warming claim that the carbon dioxide levels found in ice cores at various depths indicate that the earth is getting warmer. *National Geographic* devoted 74 pages on global warming in September of 2004. The very first data presentation (page 20) indicates that the CO_2 concentration in the atmosphere was practically flat (unchanged) until very recently; obviously man-induced. However, if you waded through the next 45 pages, you would find another chart discussing "astronomical rhythms." By comparing the chart on page 20 pertaining to carbon dioxide and temperature data to the one on page 65 pertaining to astronomical rhythms (which few people would think to do), you will notice that the first chart on page 20 represents only 0.25 percent of this ice core data! Further examination shows that this "rapid increase" in temperature and carbon dioxide occurs multiple times in the past and is unrelated to man. A graph of the complete carbon dioxide data from the Vostok Antarctic ice core (provided by NOAA) is shown in figure #5. "PPM" stands for parts per mil-lion; "300 PPM" equals 0.03 percent. "Evolutionary Years before Present" is based on the evolutionary model.

This idea to "interpret all data to support a theory of global warming" is fallacious thinking for a variety of reasons. It disregards other scientists' analysis indicating that the earth's temperature has gone through changes as great as 6 degrees warmer or even 12 degrees colder in a single decade! It disregards the fact that plants thrive on carbon dioxide and would be producing more oxygen. It disregards the fact that the carbon dioxide measurements of old snow and ice may not necessarily reflect the carbon dioxide level of the atmosphere for that time. (For example, a single volcano eruption can cause the temperature of the earth to decrease by more than one degree.) It disregards the fact that microbes may significantly alter the carbon dioxide levels at different depths of the ice cores. It disregards the fact that the depth of the ice core and the age of the ice core are determined by gross assumptions. It disregards the fact that some ancient ice cores show extreme variations of carbon dioxide that far surpass the estimates of the human-produced carbon dioxide of the past 100 years. For example, the current carbon dioxide concentration in the atmosphere is believed to be about 350 parts per million (ppm), yet the Vostok Antarctic ice core data above indicates that the carbon dioxide level 20,000 years ago (by their convoluted age-measurement scheme) was only 180 parts per million! Therefore, the Vostok Antarctic ice core indicates that the carbon dioxide level began to rapidly increase thousands of years before man's widespread use of fossil fuels. Furthermore, this ice core data indicates that the temperature was 20 degrees colder at that time and that this happened multiple times in the past. Is this data valid at all? Most plant life is severely crippled at carbon dioxide concentration levels as low as 220 and would be dead at this cold temperature with a carbon dioxide level of only 150. The carbon dioxide levels dropped dangerously low, below 200 PPM, four times according to this data. Are we to believe that life, as we know it, practically died out four times in the past? To sum up the ice core argument in a single statement — it disregards the facts. It has no foundation. For this reason, even proponents of global warming often disregard ice core data.

Sea Ice and Glacier Melt

The one *evidence* that proponents of global warming seem to articulate the loudest and most often is the melting of sea ice and glaciers. In this section, we will show that although some sea ice has broken up recently and glaciers in general seem to be shrinking, this may have nothing to do with global warming.

On a global basis, most glaciers appear to be shrinking. However, some glaciers are growing larger. For example, six P-38 Lightning fighter planes and two B-17 Flying Fortress bombers crash-landed in Greenland on July 15, 1942, and are now buried under 250 feet of ice. Nevertheless, more glaciers appear to be shrinking than growing. To the casual observer, a melting glacier means a warmer climate; therefore, the earth must be getting warmer. To the casual observer — the common person listening to the media — this makes sense. To a meteorologist, this makes no sense at all. Glaciers exist in subfreezing climates. A slight temperature difference of a fraction of a degree will have virtually no effect on whether it is growing or shrinking. Also notice, glaciers do not exist in every subfreezing climate. Glaciers form and grow larger in areas where the snowfall of the winter exceeds the

GREENLAND

BE-2

BW-8

crash site

BW-1

P-38

B-17

melting of the
summer. Glaciers
shrink in areas
where the snowfall
of the winter is less
than the melting of the summer. Consequently, whether a glacier
is growing or shrinking is a function of local "weather patterns,"
not a global temperature change of less than one degree.

One could just as easily argue that shrinking glaciers
provide evidence of cooling, not warming. Cooler air carries less
moisture which would contribute to less snowfall in the winter and
therefore — *voila* — shrinking glaciers. Does this sound farfetched?
As mentioned in the beginning of this chapter, in the 1970s, cooling was a major concern. Citing two examples:

- *Science Magazine*, March 1, 1975, stated "an ice age is
  a real possibility."

- *Science Digest*, February 1973: "Once the freeze starts,
  it will be too late."

Also, the IPCC uses the shrinking glacier story as its primary proof positive for global warming. Yet one adverse result of global warming, according to this same study, is that "increases in the amount of precipitation are *very likely* in high latitudes. . . ." (The dominant portion of high-latitude precipitation is, of course, snow.) This "glacier story" is therefore

    (a) counter-intuitive, and
    (b) contradictory.

It is *counter-intuitive* because warmer air is likely to cause an increase in glacier size, and it is *contradictory* because they use shrinking glaciers as their proof positive for global warming!

With all this conjecture of increasing or decreasing temperatures and growing and shrinking glaciers, it is absolutely important to acknowledge a biblical perspective. According to Genesis 7:11 and 8:2, the "fountains of the deep" erupted during the Flood. These fountains could very well have been sub-marine volcanoes. Due to this substantial sub-marine volcanic activity, the Ice Age would be a natural phenomenon to follow after the Flood for centuries. The warmer waters would have caused substantial precipitation during the Flood and for years afterward. This would have caused glaciers to form very rapidly and massively. According to God's Word, the Flood was only about 4,500 years ago — not tens of thousands and certainly not millions of years ago. One thing is certain: the glaciers we see today did not exist prior to the Flood. Therefore, they are actually very young. It is quite possible that our receding glaciers are, to this day, evidence of a world still recovering from the Genesis Flood.

What is also disturbing about these glacier stories is the choice of data interpretation to fit the story. For example, some lakes in Siberia are getting larger, supposedly due to the melting of glaciers. However, other lakes are getting smaller. Could it be just natural cycles? No, the smaller lakes are supposedly shrinking because the permafrost beneath them has melted and they are draining. There is no evidence to support this notion. According to the global warming alarmists, growing lakes and shrinking lakes both support their cause. This is obviously just conjecture formulated to fit the global warming scenario.

Along with the glacier stories, one will also hear of massive ice shelves breaking and falling into the sea. Once again, to the casual observer, this may appear to be evidence of *warming*. The truth is — this is evidence of cooling temperatures. As the temperatures cool, more and more seawater freezes and the ice shelves grow larger. These ice shelves grow longer and stretch out into the sea farther. However, the tidal forces continue to lift and relax, lift and relax against the underside of these shelves. Eventually the surface area of the underside of the shelf combined with the increased cantilever effect of the long shelf cause the shelf to break. The Larsen B Antarctic ice shelf that broke in February 2002 had a surface area of 2,200 square miles, which is almost the size of Delaware! The fact that the shelf grew so large is evidence of cooling temperatures. Once again, even the IPCC report confirms this.

We also hear of the reduced Arctic ice. This reduced ice is portrayed once again as a result of global warming and is your fault for driving a car. The facts that (a) ocean currents have more to do with arctic ice than surface air temperatures, and (b) the sleeping arctic volcanoes have recently awakened with enormous energy releases are completely overlooked.

Weather Extremes

Droughts, floods, hurricanes, and cyclones: we constantly hear of extreme weather conditions all over the world. We hear dire warnings like "Flee Hurricane Ike or face certain death, officials warn." To be politically correct, we must assume that these are a direct result of global warming. However, is this true? In this section, we will discuss these "extreme weather" patterns and show that they also have little to do with global warming.

We have experienced all of these extreme weather patterns throughout history. The Bible speaks of countless extreme weather patterns. Were these also a result of global warming? As the story

goes, we are having more extreme weather patterns. Are we? Do you think that the media's insatiable appetite for sensationalism may have something to do with the perception of increased weather extremes? This was a common question after Hurricane Katrina in 2005. Hurricanes themselves were a topic of much debate. According to proponents of global warming, the number and size of hurricanes should be clearly increasing. Can you name a significant hurricane since Hurricane Katrina? The United States has seen substantially fewer hurricanes and significantly less damage since Katrina. So, is the frequency of hurricanes actually increasing? By listening to the media reports, you would think that the storms are getting noticeably worse practically every year. Dr. Larry Vardiman studied this subject in depth and plotted the number of storms per year between 1851 and 2005. According to this report, *Are Hurricanes Getting More Destructive?*, there has been an increase, but not that you could notice without closely examining very de-

Number of storms per year

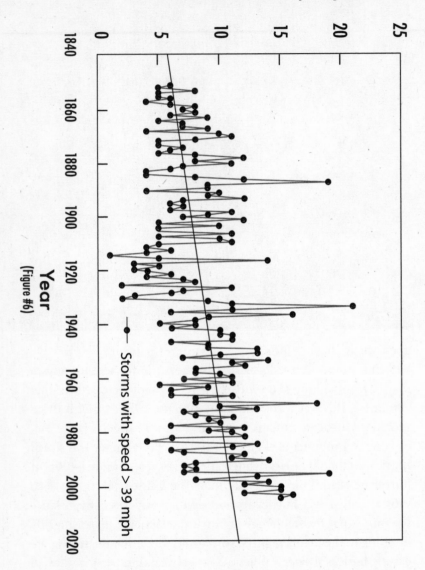

Year
(Figure #6)

Storms with speed > 39 mph

tailed data (figure #6). There has been an increase, but at a rate of increase of five storms over 150 years; that is only one storm per 30 years! Can you remember any storms 30 years ago? Obviously, this is not a "noticeable" change.

As mentioned earlier, Hurricane Katrina killed over 1,800 people and caused over 80 billion dollars of destruction. Hurricanes may very well be getting more destructive. But, is it because the storms are getting worse? The data suggests not. Or is it because our coastlines are rapidly becoming more populated? With higher population densities along the coasts, even small storms can be terribly destructive. Hurricane Ike of 2008 was a mere category 2 when it hit Galveston, yet it caused enormous damage due to the population density on such a low lying area.

Since Hurricane Katrina, subsequent hurricanes have been infrequent and mild. But the media continues to broadcast every little event. Every natural disaster anywhere in the world now seems to be considered a "man-made" disaster. It is amazing how even earthquakes and volcanoes get mixed into the conversation of extreme climate patterns and become associated with man-made global warming.

The hurricane frequency data, as Dr. Vardiman and other scientists have reported, is an interesting way to "test the theory." Are there any other ways that we can test this global warming theory?

Testing the Theory

Perhaps the best way to evaluate whether or not global warming is actually real is to test the theory. The IPCC has made climate projections based on expectations of future greenhouse gas emissions. Suppose we use the same science to make climate projections but introduce these projections based on 1979 data. This way we can test the theory by looking at "cause" and "projected effect," then compare it with actual historical data. As we look at this chart (as determined by George C. Marshall Institute), we compare actual temperature data where the bottom line represents average temperature to the upper line representing the IPCC projections. According to this test (figure #7), the global warming hypothesis fails.

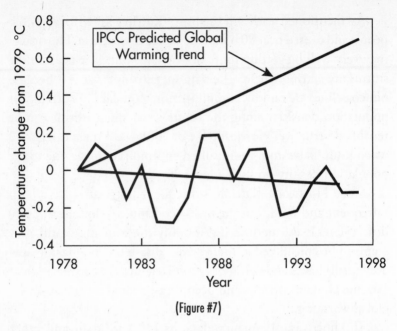

(Figure #7)

By this time you may be asking, "If long-term temperature data is not even possible to obtain, ice core data lacks a factual basis, glacier and ice shelf evidence is counter-intuitive and contradictory, and scientific climate change projections fail, what evidence is there to support global warming?" Why do you ask for *evidence*? Remember — global warming is *assumed*. Man burns fossil fuels (those carbon remains of life before the Flood). This produces carbon dioxide that causes the temperature of the earth to increase. (And so the story goes.) Who needs evidence?

Atmospheric Stability

From a secular point of view, this logic is not entirely unfounded. Everything we know about the earth tells us that the atmosphere is extremely stable. Our ecosystem is enormous and has been designed such that adverse events have natural occurring counter effects that keep the atmosphere in balance. However, if we look at the geological records (including ice cores), obviously some very violent events took place. With this in mind, we have two worldviews:

Evolutionary View	Biblical View
If we believe in evolutionary uniformitarian processes, then we must believe that despite all our data of an extremely stable atmosphere, it must actually be very fragile.	On the other hand, with a biblical view of the geologic record, we recognize that the violent events are a direct result of the Flood described in Genesis 7–9.

There are a couple of scientific theories to describe the events of the Flood, but it will suffice to say in this book, this was a single event that was prescribed by God Himself. The massive sedimentary deposits and the Ice Age were a direct result of what we often refer to as Noah's flood. The unshakable stability of the earth's atmosphere and the violent evidence recorded in the geological record are completely consistent with a biblical view of the world around us.

The Smoking Gun

As mentioned before, "Extraordinary claims require extraordinary evidence to support such claims." So far, the burden of proof to provide that extraordinary evidence has fallen squarely on the shoulders of the proponents of global warming, and they have failed miserably. Their presuppositions of global warming fall primarily in the areas of conjecture and data that is impossible for the common man to verify. But not all data is impossible for us to verify. In this section, we will present easily verifiable temperature data that indicates that the earth is not getting any warmer.

The United States is not exactly a small nation. In terms of area, it is the third largest country in the world, representing over 3.7 million square miles. It may not be large enough to provide an average temperature that represents the entire world, but it is certainly large enough to provide timing information regarding record highs and record low temperatures. If the earth is actually getting warmer, as proponents of global warming suggest, there should clearly be an increasing number of record highs and a decreasing number of record lows. This is something that is easy to verify. The data below came from the U.S. National Climatic Data Center (last updated in August of 2006) as reported on USAToday. com. Let's first examine the record low temperatures.

State	Temp (F)	Date
Delaware	-17	January 17, 1893
Ohio	-39	February 10, 1899
Nebraska	-47	February 12, 1899
Florida	-2	February 13, 1899
Louisiana	-16	February 13, 1899
New Jersey	-34	January 5, 1904
Pennsylvania	-42	January 5, 1904
Kansas	-40	February 13, 1905
Missouri	-40	February 13, 1905
Maryland	-40	January 13, 1912
Tennessee	-32	December 30, 1917
West Virginia	-37	December 30, 1917
Maine	-48	January 19, 1925
Oklahoma	-27	January 18, 1930
Texas	-23	February 8, 1933
Wyoming	-66	February 9, 1933
Oregon	-54	February 10, 1933
Vermont	-50	December 30, 1933
New Hampshire	-47	January 29, 1934
Michigan	-51	February 9, 1934
North Dakota	-60	February 15, 1936
South Dakota	-58	February 17, 1936
Nevada	-50	January 8, 1937
California	-45	January 20, 1937
Georgia	-17	January 27, 1940
Connecticut	-32	January 16, 1943
Idaho	-60	January 18, 1943
New Mexico	-50	January 1, 1951
Montana	-70	January 20, 1954
Alabama	-27	January 30, 1966
Mississippi	-19	January 31, 1966
Washington	-48	December 30, 1968
Arizona	-40	January 7, 1971
Alaska	-80	January 23, 1971
New York	-52	February 18, 1979
Hawaii	12	May 17, 1979

State	Temp (F)	Date
Massachusetts	-35	January 12, 1981
North Carolina	-34	January 21, 1985
South Carolina	-19	January 21, 1985
Virginia	-30	January 22, 1985
Colorado	-61	February 1, 1985
Utah	-69	February 1, 1985
Indiana	-36	January 19, 1994
Kentucky	-37	January 19, 1994
Minnesota	-60	February 2, 1996
Iowa	-47	February 3, 1996
Wisconsin	-55	February 4, 1996
Rhode Island	-25	February 5, 1996
Illinois	-36	January 5, 1999
Arkansas	-29	February 13, 2005

If the United States is in fact getting warmer, there should be significantly fewer record lows in the latter years than in the earlier years. This is not the case. No significant indication of "fewer low temperatures" exists. In fact, 14 of the record lows have occurred since 1980. There have been 18 record low temperatures since 1970. How does this compare with the record high temperatures?

State	Temp (F)	Date
Colorado	118	July 11, 1888
Oregon	119	August 10, 1898
Vermont	105	July 4, 1911
New Hampshire	106	July 4, 1911
Maine	105	July 10, 1911
California	134	July 10, 1913
Alaska	100	June 27, 1915
Alabama	112	September 5, 1925
New York	108	July 22, 1926
Delaware	110	July 21, 1930
Kentucky	114	July 28, 1930
Mississippi	115	July 29, 1930
Tennessee	113	August 9, 1930
Hawaii	100	April 27, 1931

State	Temp (F)	Date
Florida	109	June 29, 1931
Iowa	118	July 20, 1934
Ohio	113	July 21, 1934
Idaho	118	July 28, 1934
Minnesota	114	July 6, 1936
Maryland	109	July 10, 1936
New Jersey	110	July 10, 1936
Pennsylvania	111	July 10, 1936
West Virginia	112	July 10, 1936
Michigan	112	July 13, 1936
Wisconsin	114	July 13, 1936
Indiana	116	July 14, 1936
Nebraska	118	July 24, 1936
Kansas	121	July 24, 1936
Louisiana	114	August 10, 1936
Arkansas	120	August 10, 1936
Texas	120	August 12, 1936
North Dakota	110	August 21, 1936
Montana	117	July 5, 1937
Georgia	112	July 24, 1952
South Carolina	111	June 28, 1954
Illinois	117	July 14, 1954
Missouri	118	July 14, 1954
Virginia	110	July 15, 1954
Washington	118	August 5, 1961
Rhode Island	104	August 2, 1975
Massachusetts	107	August 2, 1975
Wyoming	116	August 8, 1983
North Carolina	110	August 21, 1983
Utah	117	July 5, 1985
Oklahoma	120	June 27, 1994
New Mexico	122	June 27, 1994
Nevada	125	June 29, 1994
Arizona	128	June 29, 1994
Connecticut	106	July 15, 1995
South Dakota	120	July 15, 2006

As you can see from the previous table, there were only 9 record-high temperatures since 1980 and only 11 since 1970. This is truly a smoking gun for the proponents of global warming.

There have been 50 to 60 percent more record lows in the past few decades than record highs. According to Al Gore, the global warming alarmist's greatest salesman, "The ten hottest years on record were in the last 14 years."[3] According to the data on page 72-74, the United States, the third largest country in the world, is getting colder.

This is a profound observation. One criticism of global temperature measurements earlier in this chapter was that no worldwide-standardized temperature measurements existed until 1968. However, the data on page 72-74 circumvents that concern. The comparison of record highs and record lows pertains to temperature measurements observed in a single country by relatively standard measurement techniques since 1970. The data may be limited in geographic area, but it includes 50 different states with common temperature measurement techniques that predate the international standards. If the world is getting warmer, our most recent decades should certainly be showing us more record high temperatures than record low temperatures. However, the data clearly illustrates the exact opposite—that there have been more record low temperatures than record highs. Perhaps the 1970s warnings of an impending ice age are credible after all!

Not convinced? Check out Australia. Australia is diagonally across the globe. It is nearly the size of the United States and is the sixth largest country in the world, with a landmass of nearly three million square miles. According to Geoscience Australia (an agency of the Australian Government), the all-time record high was well over 100 years ago in 1889. The all-time record low was very recently, in 1994.

Ulterior Motives

This brings us to the first motive behind the global-warming hysteria — an assault on God's Word, the Bible. If the politicians, media, and worshipers of "mother earth" (Rom. 1:25) can get you to fall for this tale of global warming, they have succeeded

---

3. From the advertising trailer for the movie *An Inconvenient Truth*.

in eroding your faith in the foundation of His Word. They have distracted your mind and diverted your attention away from the truths of Genesis 7–9 and undermined a portion of your faith. Like our introductory illustration of David and Goliath, any diversion from your mission of serving and glorifying God undermines your walk with Him. This is only the beginning of the dangers of this hysteria.

There are actually multiple motives behind promoting this global warming hysteria. The people who promote global warming are extremely diverse in culture and ideologies. They may disagree on every other aspect of life, but the one thing they have in common is a concern about global warming. Why is this? The next few paragraphs will discuss these various motives.

First of all, if global warming is so bogus, why do so many scientists support it? Don't these folks in white lab coats merely report their findings in an unbiased, pragmatic manner? That depends. Many do. Perhaps we should ask whether or not we are hearing about all the scientific data that indicates that the earth is not warming. Remember, this is more a media war more than a scientific war. Also, what was the purpose of the funding for the global warming research? If it was driven by efforts to "better understand" global warming, then by the mere nature of the scope of the project, it will support the theory. This funding issue is crucial. Scientists do not have funding to research anything they want. To get funding quickly, scare tactics are often highly effective. They need to seek funding for specific reasons. With all the media and political hype on global warming, there is significant funding on the subject. On the other hand, try to find funding for objective research on the subject. That would be difficult to find because it is not "politically correct." Scientists who would like to provide non-biased research find considerable difficulty with funding. Furthermore, this is such a political issue that job security can be threatened if scientists attempt to swim against the current. This is not just true in the sciences but is a cold, cruel reality of any occupation. Lastly, there is no such thing as "no bias." We all have opinions and biases. The many different reasons that scientists use to choose the particular bias they have is just as variable as anyone else's bias and can be steered by any of the following reasons.

One very simple motive is merely to satisfy our desire for purpose in life. God had a purpose in mind for you before you were even born (see Ps. 139:16). It is His desire that everyone should come to know Him and spend eternal life with Him (see 2 Pet. 3:9). Unbelievers have obviously missed this purpose that God had intended. There is absolutely nothing they can do that will please God (Rom. 8:8), but that does not eliminate the God-given desire to seek a purpose. Consequently, unbelievers will often fall for causes that appear to be righteous according to their own well-intended understanding (see Prov. 3:5). They are not out to be vicious or malicious, but they have fallen into the hands of Satan. These people cannot understand why everyone is not actively concerned about global warming. After all, anyone with a sense of right and wrong should act with a sense of environmental responsibility.

The next group of people is a bit more cunning and considerably more dangerous. We will discuss this in greater detail in the next chapter, but if the world is gradually warming, there is practically nothing man can do about it — even if everyone does everything they possibly can. This being the case, it provides a perfect never-ending, self-serving political platform for politicians with no genuine platform. This issue is unsolvable, so it will be around forever. Since no solution exists, the politician needs only to raise the issue, not provide solutions. Because actual long-term temperature measurements are not possible, it cannot be proved or disproved, so no one can destroy the platform. And finally, it seems like a worthy cause; no responsible person would vote for destroying the earth. After all, those who are not in favor of taking care of this planet must be irresponsible sub-citizens. In this world of political correctness, dissenters of environmentalism are considered ignorant, dishonest, or at a bare minimum have no credibility. This is a very dangerous effect of the global warming hysteria. It provides an appearance of credibility to politicians who have no credibility. It also provides the appearance of a valid platform for ungodly, irresponsible legislation. "Credibility" for politicians should involve "solutions" not just "criticism." Anyone can criticize. True political credibility includes offering legitimate solutions. Not one has been offered. We will discuss the lack of credibility of most of the so-called solutions to the global warming issue in the next chapter.

To discuss the next motive of the proponents of this global warming hysteria, we first need to step back 30 to 40 years in our history. In the 60s, 70s, and 80s, "Public Enemy #1" was *communism*. What is communism? Communism is an ideology that seeks to destroy capitalism. They want to destroy capitalism because it is their ideology that the poor are poor because the rich are rich. Their solution would be to make the rich become poor. That way, the poor will have more. The supposed solutions to global warming (which we will discuss in the next chapter) will also serve to cripple the capitalist societies. As you will recall, this Communist ideology was not unique to the Soviet Union and Eastern world. It existed in Western Europe and the United States, too. Then two events changed all of that. The Berlin Wall was destroyed in 1989, and Boris Yeltsin brought an end to the Soviet style of communism in 1991. From that point on, for the most part communism became unfashionable and temporarily went into hibernation. That is, until recently. This same ideology is now disguised in the politically correct form of — you guessed it — the global warming ideology. This ideology can now promote the destruction of capitalism and industrialization under the guise of righteous environmentalism! This is, of course, an extremely destructive godless ideology. The perfect crime is often erroneously considered to be one where no evidence is left behind. The truth is, the perfect crime is actually a crime where the victim believes he has been served a favor. From this respect, these Communist proponents of global warming are committing the "perfect crime."

The next group of people to support the concept of global warming are those with potential financial gain. Along with the scare tactics of global warming comes a whole suite of new products. These products may be as small as an "Energy Star" qualified light bulb or as big as a new house with better insulation. These products could also include home electronics, appliances, heating and air conditioning units, doors and windows, solar panels, windmills, and the list goes on. Advertising campaigns are full of "new more efficient products." Purchasing these items can be productive, or it can be a total waste of money. Unfortunately, it is often difficult to determine to what extent these products will really help. We will discuss some of these in the next chapter.

And lastly, there is the Christian element. Yes, even Christians promote this ideology (reference: *The Evangelical Climate Initiative*). Unfortunately, even some high-profile, well-respected Christian leaders have fallen for this hype. This is quite sad because many of the godless people with the motives discussed previously would love to fragment the Christian community. Christians rightfully have a sense of stewardship toward God's provisions. This is a good thing. Christians need to channel that desire for good stewardship in a manner that is productive, scripturally sound, and based firmly on His Word.

Political Correctness

In the previous section we discussed the fact that "pressures" are exerted on professionals to report politically correct data. The idea that the information with which we make important decisions may be less than accurate is quite disturbing. This is the United States, not the Soviet Union. We do not employ a "disinformation agency." Is this really an issue?

This was indeed the very subject of Ben Stein's controversial documentary *Expelled*. Mr. Stein documents multiple scientists who have not just been pressured but have lost their jobs by not sticking to the politically correct agenda. Mr. Stein was prophetic when he stated before the release of the film that opponents would twist his words. He took great care to articulate his case very clearly. Yet the negative reviews of the film attacked it based on false quotes. For example, they accused Mr. Stein of denying the Holocaust, claiming that he stated the Holocaust did not happen. How absurd. The statement he made was quite the opposite: that no one would dare teach his or her children that the Holocaust did not happen. This is just one example of blatant deception regarding this documentary. Mr. Stein also clearly separated "intelligent design" from "creationism." His documentary dealt with intelligent design, not creationism. There are clear distinctions. Yet his opponent's biggest objection was that he was addressing creationism. That's a pretty lame defense. Even if these people were proponents of creationism, should they lose their jobs because of a religious conviction? The point is still exactly the same; they were persecuted because of their lack of political correctness.

The global warming issue is no different. On September 20, 2005, one month after Hurricane Katrina, Max Mayfield, the director of the National Hurricane Center (a part of NOAA's National Weather Service), testified before Congress that "The increased activity since 1995 is due to natural fluctuations (and) cycles of hurricane activity driven by the Atlantic Ocean itself along with the atmosphere above it and not enhanced substantially by global warming." The uproar over that statement from this highly respected official was practically deafening. We should first look at his credentials. According to www.noaa.gov, Mr. Mayfield is a Fellow of the American Meteorological Society. In 1996 The America Meteorological Society honored him with the Francis W. Reichelderfer Award. He also received an Outstanding Achievement Award at the 2000 National Hurricane Conference. In 2004, he received the Richard Hagemeyer Award.

Max Mayfield

After Hurricane Katrina, Mr. Mayfield was named ABC Television Network's "Person of the Week." He received a Presidential Rank Award for Meritorious Service in 2005. Mr. Mayfield received gold medals from the U.S. Department of Commerce for his work during Hurricane Andrew (1992) and Hurricane Isabel (2003), and a Silver Medal during Hurricane Gilbert (1988). NOAA awarded him a bronze medal for his work in disaster preparedness. Currently, Mr. Mayfield is the chairman of the World Meteorological Organization's Regional Association-IV, supporting 26 countries. Had it not been for Mr. Mayfield's personal call to New Orleans Mayor Ray Nagin, expressing the urgency of evacuation, the Katrina death toll could have easily been 10 to 100 times higher. Mr. Mayfield is one of the most decorated authorities on hurricanes, yet with all these credentials and awards, within days of his statement on global warming, environmental groups and NOAA officials were calling for his immediate resignation.

Has global warming become a religious topic? Absolutely. It has little to do with science and is based on what we *believe*. We will discuss that later in the next chapter. But people do not have to have a religious platform to be pressured by political correctness. Few people brave the ridicule of speaking out against global-warming alarmism. Fortunately, prominent public figures are now speaking out.

John Coleman, the founder of the cable TV Weather Channel in 1982 and weathercaster for 50 years, claims that global warming "is the greatest scam in history" and that we are being told what to think. "This is my field of lifelong expertise. And I am telling you global warming is a non-event, a manufactured crisis, and a total scam" (ICECAP, Nov. 7, 2007).

Dr. Joseph D'Aleo was the first director of meteorology at the cable TV Weather Channel. Dr. D'Aleo has over 30 years experience in professional meteorology and is a Fellow of the American Meteorological Society (AMS). He has served as co-chair and chairman of AMS committees and then was elected councilor for the AMS. Dr. D'Aleo was also a professor of meteorology at Lyndon State College and speaks out against global-warming alarmism, saying that the role of the oceans is greatly underestimated and that the oceans correlate far better than any other factor. He believes that the media helps distort the picture because sensationalism is what sells.[4] Dr. D'Aleo claims that a recent significant drop in temperature driven by a rapid reversal from El Niño to La Niña is proof of the substantial effects of ocean currents.

The enormously popular president of the Czech Republic is also an avid opponent of global-warming alarmism. Vaclav Klaus calls man-made global warming "a myth" and insists that the IPCC is not a scientific institution but a political body with a "one-sided opinion and a one-sided assignment." He also made a very profound statement: "It's clear that the poorer the society is, the

---

4. http://www.appliedforecasting.com/index.php?option=com_content&task=view&id=551&Itemid=32

more brutally it behaves with respect to nature, and vice versa."[5] Yet it is not the poorer societies being pressured to change. It is the wealthier societies that are being urged to cripple themselves with environmental changes that will destroy their economies. Who will support the poorer societies when the wealthier ones undergo economic collapse? Mr. Klaus is so convinced that man-made global warming is a myth that he has published a book entitled *Blue Planet in Green Shackles*. In his address to the National Press Club on May 27, 2008, he stated, "My today's thinking is substantially influenced by the fact that I spent most of my life under the Communist regime which ignored and brutally violated human freedom and wanted to command not only the people but also the nature." He continues, "My central concern is — in a condensed form — captured in the subtitle of this book. I ask: 'What is Endangered: Climate or Freedom?' " Mr. Klaus clearly understands what is at stake. He was born on June 19, 1941, and lived in Communist Czechoslovakia until the Velvet Revolution that formed the Czech Republic in 1989. If any current-day politician understands the meaning of government propaganda, it is Vaclav Klaus. He elaborates:

> I do not, however, live in the past and do not see the future threats to free society coming from the old and old-fashioned Communist ideology. The name of the new danger will undoubtedly be different, but its substance will be very similar. There will be the same attractive, to a great extent pathetic and at first sight quasi-noble idea that transcends the individual in the name of something above him (of something greater than his poor self), supplemented by enormous self-confidence on the side of those who stand behind it. Like their predecessors, they will be certain that they have the right to sacrifice man and his freedom to make their idea reality. In the past it was in the name of

---

5. http://www.drudgereportarchives.com/data/2007/02/12/20070212_161315_flash.htm

the masses (or of the Proletariat), this time in the name of the Planet. Structurally, it is very similar.

His views on the future are very prophetic, as we will see in the next chapter.

Chapter 5

Projected Future of Global Conditions (Global Warming)

And God blessed them, and God said unto them, Be fruitful, and multiply, and replenish the earth, and subdue it: and have dominion over the fish of the sea, and over the fowl of the air, and over every living thing that moveth upon the earth (Gen. 1:28).

I n this chapter, we will explore the projected global conditions from environmental, economic, and spiritual perspectives. We will first discuss the gross misconceptions of the environmental aspects of this global-warming hysteria. We need to lay down the rumors and size up the facts before us.

Our two characters are still standing in the middle of a valley. Thousands of soldiers, fraught with anticipation, are standing on the hillsides waiting to see what will happen next. The small young man looks at the very large warrior. He notices his helmet of brass, his coat of mail that must have weighed 125 pounds, the brass on his legs, and the "target" between his shoulders. *This fellow is so big and carrying so much weight that he can hardly move,* the small young man thought. *He has an opening in his helmet that is just large enough for one of these stones. With the Lord's help, I could run right towards him and sling one of these stones right into his forehead.*

Who Controls the Weather?

Certainly not "Goliath." Consider Genesis 6–9 (Noah's Flood), Genesis 41 (the seven-year famine), Exodus 7–10 (weather plagues of Egypt), and Ecclesiastes 1:7 and Job 36:27–28 (the water cycle). As we discussed in the previous chapter, God was clearly in command of the weather during Old Testament times. But what about the weather in more recent times? Consider Mark 15:33 while Jesus hung on the Cross and it became dark in the middle of the day, "from the sixth hour to the ninth hour" (about noon to 3 p.m. — much too long for an eclipse). Are these examples still too far in the past to be appreciated? Consider the following historically documented weather-related direct answers to prayer:

1. A critical rain for the Pilgrims in July of 1623 that miraculously restored a lost crop, producing a bountiful harvest that provided them with enough food to save them from starvation through the next winter, according to William Bradford.

2. A dense fog on August 6, 1776, that permitted George Washington and his troops to escape a siege of 800 troops on Long Island.

3. Perhaps one of the most noteworthy weather-related experiences ever was the destruction of a French armada of 70 ships and 13,000 men in 1746 during the reign of King Louis XV under the command of the Duke of d'Anville. This fleet was sent to "teach a lesson" to the British colonies. One by one, each ship was lost at sea or run aground due to severe weather consisting of wind and dense fogs while crossing the Atlantic or during the first couple of weeks of October trying to regroup for the series of attacks. The armada grouped and regrouped, but each time, the ships and men were lost by disease, wind, and fog. Eventually the remaining troops on one warship, *la Sirène*, sailed back to France to report to the king how the British colonies stood still, defeating the 70-ship armada without firing a single shot.

The God of Noah, Joseph, Moses, Solomon, and Job, as well as the God of William Bradford, the Duke of d'Anville, and George Washington is the same great and omnipotent God of today. Your weatherman does not control the weather. No man has that ability. If God can cause such direct interaction of the weather, a few parts per million of carbon dioxide is not too much for Him to handle.

Transportation Solutions

However, according to some hypothetical committee of the elusive "they," the solution to global warming seems to be very simple — stop using fossil fuels that produce carbon dioxide. But the "cure" to this disease called "global warming" is clearly far worse than the disease itself. As Christians with a proper stewardship obligation to our Creator, we need to evaluate this question objectively. God could have totally obliterated the remains from Noah's flood, but He chose not to. Could it be that He stored those for our future use? The media would have us believe that we are to stop using them and that there are all sorts of simple solutions right on the horizon, if we are just willing to go there. We are told that some of these "solutions" are not fully feasible yet, but the little details will be resolved by our masterful technology in just a few short years. We are expected to believe that since we are the culprits of this predicament, we must pay the price to resolve it.

However, as responsible Christians, we cannot fall for half-baked ideas. We must understand one thing in order to keep this in perspective: scientists have been aggressively searching for cleaner alternative practical sources of energy for over 30 years. The early 1970s experienced a rapid increase in energy prices due to problems in the Middle East. Sound familiar? When considering the effects of inflation, it has only been very recently that energy prices have reached the previous all-time high of the 1970s. However, that energy crisis was a serious wake-up call for the United States. Solutions to global dependence on foreign oil (primarily Middle Eastern) have been a national priority ever since. Unfortunately, the scientific results are still bleak. With very minor exceptions, very little progress has been made in these areas. The legitimate potential progress that was initiated in the 1970s has been obtained. There is little more we can do to tweak existing technologies. Short of discovering totally new technologies, our energy situation will improve very little. This is "the Land of Opportunity." If a scientist truly found a viable, cost-effective, clean source of energy, he would not only become an instant hero, he would become very wealthy very quickly. No conspiracy of hundreds of corporations all around the world in the energy business would be able to quiet this discovery. The forward-thinking executives would be clamoring to license this new invention or discovery. They would have no choice. To ignore it could be the end of their business.

There are numerous gross misconceptions about the so-called solutions. Automobiles certainly contribute significantly to the production of carbon dioxide. They are also very personal. We use them daily, and they are often not just means of transportation but also statements of our personalities, so let's look closely at four automotive concepts that are touted as potential solutions. There may be practical applications for any of these concepts, but their impact on alleged global warming is limited. To evaluate them, we will need to have an understanding of how they work and the sciences involved with their effectiveness or limitations.

Hybrid Vehicles

This is a classic example of what rumors and skewed thinking can do to a normally sensible rational market. We hear claims that "hybrid auto technology simply transfers railroad locomotive hybrid technology to the common automobile." Or, "The hybrid technology is so efficient that the military is considering using it on their combat vehicles." There is so much confusion about the hybrid technology that we will address this from several different perspectives. However, before we address the locomotive and military vehicles, let's first discuss hybrid automobiles.

People spend $5,000 or more for a vehicle with significantly lower performance than the conventional counterpart. Is this truly what they intended? Or do they fully understand the hybrid technology? Let's look at the difference between two comparable vehicles — one hybrid and one conventional.

QUALITY & VALUE ANALYSIS		
Model	2008 Honda Civic Hybrid CV Transmission	2008 Honda Civic Sedan DX 5-Spd MT
Comparably Equipped Price	$23,235	$15,645
5-year Repair & Maint. Costs	$2,056	$1,806
Engine	i-VTEC® 1.3LI4	1.8L I4

The information in the previous chart comes directly from the manufacturer's advertising. It is not the point to criticize the manufacturer. (We could just as easily compared the Toyota Prius to the Toyota Yaris.) They are merely supplying a vehicle for a real market. The MSRP price of the hybrid vehicle is over $7,500 more than the conventional counterpart. What is not included in the manufacturer's information is the engine performance. According to outside testing, the 0 to 60 mph acceleration of the hybrid is 11.8 seconds compared to 7.9 seconds for the conventional vehicle! What is going on here? It is true that the hybrid gets better gas mileage than the conventional, but this is primarily due to the tiny engine of the hybrid: 1.3 liters as opposed to 1.8 liters.

The engines of these vehicles charge a battery so that the vehicle can also operate on electricity instead of the engine. Supposedly, these vehicles are more efficient than standard combustion engine vehicles. But is this true? Let's look at the basic differences:

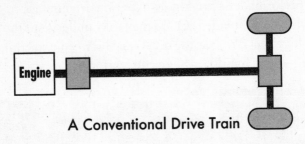

A Conventional Drive Train

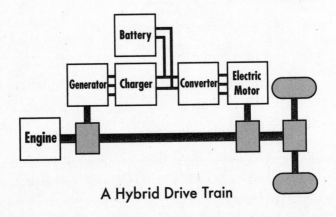

A Hybrid Drive Train

Notice that all of the additional items of the hybrid vehicle "use" energy. None of them "produce" energy. (The battery only "stores" energy.) *All* of the energy to propel this vehicle still comes from the engine — the same engine that produces carbon dioxide. There is no other source of power. Batteries can be very efficient when only slightly discharged, but become terribly inefficient when significantly discharged. Since weight is a critical factor for gas mileage of all automobiles, hybrid vehicles limit their battery size to reduce weight and rely on significant discharge rates. These vehicles would be horribly inefficient except for the fact that they can electronically recover a portion of energy when the driver steps on the brakes. The EPA miles per gallon (MPG) ratings for hybrids (through the 2007 model year) indicate that these vehicles are significantly more efficient than conventional vehicles, but let's examine these figures.

MPG Ratings	Hybrid		Conventional	
	Highway	City	Highway	City
2007	51	49	38	30
2008	45	40	34	26

In 2007 the EPA's MPG rating for the hybrid was nearly 50 percent higher than the conventional vehicle! But this is only because of the way these MPG ratings are obtained. These ratings are not determined by actual driving tests. That would be too dependent on the driver. These ratings are obtained by computer-controlled driving simulations on a dynamometer and then calculated by mathematical algorithms that include other factors such as vehicle weight, wind resistance, etc. Contrary to popular belief, these ratings were never intended to represent actual driving fuel consumption, but to be used as a means to compare one vehicle to another *comparable vehicle*. For this purpose, they are still fairly useful. However, hybrid vehicles were never considered when the EPA tests were devised, so their data is significantly skewed. Since they work differently, their ratings should not be compared with conventional vehicles.

The distortion of this hybrid MPG data is due to a variety of reasons, and we will not discuss them all. Nevertheless, two significant factors that were never considered in the MPG algorithm are the charge of the battery and the software controllability of the electric power. The MPG tests of the hybrid began with a fully charged battery and ended with a fully drained battery. This alone significantly distorts the data. The software also permitted the manufacturers to "tune" the electric power use to optimize fuel efficiencies for the EPA MPG tests in ways that would not reflect normal driving patterns. The 2008 MPG ratings are performed differently to help resolve some of these factors. The new 2008 rating methods include significantly more braking (to still give the hybrid an advantage), but with the new ratings, the 2008 hybrid gets only about 40 percent higher gas mileage than the conventional. This is primarily due to the fact that the conventional engine is about 40 percent larger than the hybrid engine. (See the charts on prior page.)

Keep in mind, the 2007 model and the 2008 model were identical. The MPG ratings changed because the "method" of testing changed. Auto manufacturers are merely responding to market desires. People spend considerably more money to purchase these vehicles that give them lower performance because they are misled by the media and politicians and falsely believe they are helping the environment. (They are well aware that the increased gas mileage will never pay for the difference in price.) The truth is, these vehicles are "less green" because:

1. all of the energy to propel the vehicle still comes from a fossil-fuel burning combustion engine, and

2. the additional batteries have their own aspects of significantly increased manufacturing and disposal pollution.

It is also interesting to note that the global-warming "hype" has more of an influence in the United States than many other countries. It is certainly true that most of Europe is more concerned with conservation than Americans. This is due to their limited space and higher overall population density. Yet they are not as gullible to the "hype." With European gas prices typically more than twice American prices, if hybrids truly were a viable solution, they should be considerably more popular there. However, the percentage of hybrid vehicles compared to conventional vehicles in Europe is only about half that of the United States.

The discussion above is not intended to convince you not to purchase a hybrid vehicle. We drive different vehicles for all kinds of reasons. The information above is intended to describe the impact of the "hybrid vehicle" on the environment. Yes, they use less gasoline; but this is primarily due to their small engine size. Even if you have no intentions of ever purchasing a hybrid vehicle, you may find the information above useful. If you are purchasing a previously owned vehicle and comparing their EPA MPG ratings, you need to be aware that the tests were changed for the 2008 model year. The MPG rating of a vehicle will be lower in 2008 than the exact same vehicle in 2007. This is not because of any change of the vehicle. It is a change of the way they are tested.

Now let us consider the locomotive and the military vehicles. If "hybrid technology" is so promising for them, why is it not so promising for passenger vehicles? Let's examine these two applications completely separately. First of all, a railroad locomotive is not a "hybrid." A "hybrid" can run on gasoline or electricity. A locomotive uses a "diesel electric" power scheme. The diesel engines turn a generator to produce electricity to power electric motors at the wheels. The engines never directly turn the wheels, so it is technically not a "hybrid." Locomotives use this technology because electric motors naturally provide the "starting torque" required to get this huge mass into motion. Automobiles use a transmission that would be terribly inefficient if used for the enormous mass of a train. Also, once the train reaches full speed, due to the solid steel wheels and the very low inclines of the tracks, it does not need near the same operating torque (pound for pound) as an automobile. Electric motors are also much more suitable for the high-speed applications of the train. Military hybrids are being considered for their "stealth" characteristics, not fuel economy. A hybrid, running on electric power, is considerably quieter than a large diesel engine. So, locomotives and military hybrids should never be used to justify the hybrid technology of an automobile. Their purposes and applications are entirely different.

Fuel Cells

Fuel cells burn hydrogen in a manner that produces electricity. The electricity propels the vehicle. On the surface, this sounds like the perfect solution. After all, no carbon dioxide is produced at all. Well . . . at least not by the vehicle. But where does the hydrogen come from? The hydrogen comes from one of two sources:

1. *Natural gas.* Natural gas is a "hydro-carbon." The by-product of generating hydrogen from natural gas is carbon dioxide — the same quantity of carbon dioxide as a combustion engine.

2. *Electrolysis.* This process extracts the hydrogen and the

oxygen from water (H_2O). That sounds like a clean process. However, electrolysis is performed by electricity. This "chemical reaction" requires *more energy* to generate the hydrogen than the amount of energy released in the fuel cell. This is fundamental physics and cannot be changed.

The end result is that more carbon dioxide is produced than with a conventional combustion engine. (Most electric power comes from fossil fuel power plants that emit carbon dioxide.) Consequently, production quantities of hydrogen come from natural gas.

According to the National Academies of Science, it will take 200 billion dollars between now and 2020 to provide the infrastructure to support two million fuel cell cars. That is 100 thousand dollars per car just for the infrastructure, and we haven't purchased a car yet. Two million autos may sound like a big number — until you consider that there are over 250 million on the American highways today.

Furthermore, fuel cells require nasty heavy metals to make the process work. These heavy metals will eventually end up in the junkyards. From a scientific point of view, there is no debate on this subject. When the origin of the hydrogen and the disposal of the heavy metals are considered, fuel cells are not "green." People who promote fuel cells for green purposes are simply misinformed — including politicians.

Electric Cars

Electric cars get their batteries charged from electric power plants — most of which operate on fossil fuels. Using combustion to turn a crankshaft is much more efficient than using combustion to heat steam to in turn make electricity, charge a battery, and turn an electric motor. This method generates more carbon

dioxide, not less. It is also important to note: the refuse (lead, nickel, cadmium, lithium, etc.) from used batteries is also a significant environmental hazard.

Ethanol

Undoubtedly, you have occasionally seen signs at the pump that state, "This gasoline contains up to 10 percent ethanol." Ten percent sounds like a considerable dent in the fuel problem. Ethanol comes from soy and corn that we can grow right here in the United States. But do not be taken in. This 10 percent is not intended to suggest that we can produce 10 percent of our fuel simply by growing corn and soy. The 10 percent ratio is a standard ratio that will not harm modern automobiles. However, it will harm your hip pocket in more ways than one.

Growing corn and soy, harvesting it, and then converting it to ethanol requires considerable energy. A debate roars as to whether or not ethanol production saves any energy at all. One thing is certain — it could not be cost effective without the current substantial federal subsidies. On the surface, federal subsidies may sound reasonable — using taxpayers' dollars to help with the fuel problem and the environment. However, looking deeper, there are three major problems with burning food for fuel.

1. Corn and soy are used in countless food products. Using agricultural land to grow "energy" instead of food increases the competition for production, and thus increasing food prices. The federal subsidy to produce corn and soy for ethanol raises the price of corn and soy for food, as well. According to the Bureau of Labor and Statistics, corn and soy prices rose 7.9 percent and 9.6 percent in March of 2008, while wheat escalated a whopping 145 percent over the 12-month period ending with March. The average price of a loaf of bread increased by an average of only 2 percent per year from 1998 though 2005. However, since we started seriously using food as a fuel, the price of bread has increased by 4 percent in 2006, 13 percent in 2007, and 17 percent so far in 2008. According to Lester Brown of the Earth Policy Institute, this is just the beginning of food price increases.

   "A University of Illinois economics team calculates that with oil at $50 a barrel, it is profitable — with the ethanol subsidy of 51¢ a gallon (equal to $1.43 per bushel of corn) — to convert corn into ethanol as long as the price is below $4 a bushel. But with oil at $100 a barrel, distillers can pay more than $7 a bushel for corn and still break even. If oil climbs to $140, distillers can pay $10 a bushel for corn — double the early 2008 price of $5 per bushel."[1]

   This statement was made on January 8, 2008. Since that time, oil prices have fluctuated wildly — from a high of over $140 per barrel to a sudden and dramatic decrease to below $40 a barrel.

2. We cannot grow enough corn and soy to solve any energy

---

1. http://www.earth-policy.org/Updates/2008/Update69.htm

crisis. According to David Pimental, a leading Cornell University agricultural expert, the farmland required to produce enough ethanol for one automobile for a year (11 acres) would produce a year's supply of food for seven people. Ethanol currently accounts for less than 5 percent of our gasoline consumption, which may sound significant until you also factor in that ethanol produces only two-thirds the energy of gasoline and that ethanol production (by some calculations) requires more energy to produce than what it delivers. Some reports suggest that the total energy to produce a gallon of ethanol exceeds 130,000 BTUs, yet a gallon of ethanol produces only 80,000 BTUs. This is a raging debate. Supposedly, this figure includes some transportation costs that are also required for oil production, but clearly the production of ethanol is terribly inefficient, regardless of where these figures finally settle out. Perhaps we could remove many of these arguably questionable variables and examine the distillation process alone. One gallon of crude oil produces approximately 0.6 gallons of gasoline (depending on the quality of the crude). On the other hand, corn needs substantial crushing just to retrieve the liquid that is 92 percent water. One gallon of this liquid (never mind the solids) produces only 0.08 gallons of ethanol, which still needs considerable processing to become pure enough for ethanol use in gasoline. If ethanol production were truly cost effective, ethanol producers would be using ethanol to supply that energy. Ethanol production costs nearly twice that of gasoline production: $1.74 per gallon as opposed to $0.95.

3. Perhaps most importantly, in the discussion of global warming, ethanol usage provides no reduction in greenhouse gasses whatsoever. Surprisingly, the EPA encourages the use of ethanol to reduce carbon dioxide emissions. Combustion of carbon fuels produces carbon dioxide, regardless of the source of this carbon.

By now you are probably wondering why there is so much global-warming emphasis on automobile solutions. These "solutions" are fictitious. Once again, the global warming issue as discussed in the previous chapter has nothing to do with science and everything to do with emotion and hype. People — individual citizens — drive vehicles. Focusing on our driving habits has the appearance of spreading the blame and responsibility of global warming on you and me. People pay thousands of extra dollars for hybrid vehicles (dollars that will never be recovered from fuel savings) because they falsely believe they are helping the environment. As we look into the future, people will be paying more for food and transportation. In some cases, they will be unaware that their increased expenses are a result of this global-warming hype. In other cases, they will gladly pay more, as they erroneously believe their actions are helping the environment.

Someone once said, "The perfect crime is not one where no clues are left behind. The perfect crime is where the victim believes that he has been done a favor."

Electric Power Plant Solutions

We will now shift our focus from automobiles to electrical power generation. From our discussion in chapter 1 concerning the second law of thermodynamics and entropy, it should be evident that all energy produced by power plants eventually becomes *entropy*, which is *heat*. When you turn the lights off at night, the room gets dark. This is because the energy that was producing the light is now all heat. Your electric range obviously produces heat. Your refrigerators and air conditioners actually produce heat. They "cool" by merely transferring heat from one undesirable location to another more desirable location.

The carbon dioxide produced by electric power plants is twice that which is produced by automobiles. It is crucial that we have a working understanding of this subject. The politicians that we elect will be legislating regulations that will have a substantial impact not only on your electric bill but also on your total cost of living. As conscientious Christian stewards, we need to elect officials who have responsible, viable energy plans. When it comes to an automobile, we select which brand and model to purchase. When it comes to the electric power that feeds our house, we have virtually no control over it, yet we want to ensure that this power is supplied 24 hours a day and that it is at an affordable cost. We may have preferences for particular environmental concerns, and we may have preferences for particular energy research. Hopefully you do. But, when it comes to politicians forcing power companies to make changes that threaten our livelihood and safety at home, it is vital that we understand these technologies and their impacts. Many politicians would have you believe that these multi-billion-dollar companies can simply bear the brunt of massive financial change and you will be the beneficiary. This is absurd! The only source of revenue available to a power company is their paying customers; that is, you and me. Our nation will soon need to spend many billions of dollars on power plants and the distribution infrastructure. This money needs to be spent responsibly. Every one of these dollars will be coming out of our pockets. There is no other source for these dollars. We need to have an understanding of the realities of alternative energy sources.

Once again, the media would have you falsely believe that viable cost-effective alternative energy sources are just around the corner. They would have us believe that it is the power companies that are dragging their feet. However, research for alternative sources of energy has been receiving significant exposure — and government funding — for over 30 years. The outlook for future energy resources has changed very little over these past 30 years. Perhaps the most significant change is that of fusion energy. Fusion is where atoms are joined together (as opposed to *fission* where atoms are split into two) and generate enormous energy. Thirty years ago it was believed that prototype fusion power plants would be in operation by now. This has not happened, nor is it expected anytime soon. The rest of the alternative energy sources have been recognized for thousands of years but have changed very little, as we shall see.

Solar Power

Truly the light is sweet, and a pleasant thing it is for the eyes to behold the sun (Eccles. 11:7).

Converting the energy of the sun into electricity is one alternative energy source. Many people believe that solar power is the ultimate solution. Although solar energy is certainly abundant, currently existing solar electric technologies are limited to only 3 percent efficiency (the combined efficiency of the solar cells, electronics, and the batteries). Solar cells will always reflect sunlight and dissipate energy as heat. Shiny solar cells will not absorb so much heat, but they will also reflect too much light. Dark solar cells may absorb more light, but they will also dissipate more heat. Either way, these are energy losses due to fundamental laws of physics that cannot be changed. Solar energy is also not cheap. One common misconception is that, after the equipment is purchased, the electricity is free. This is a gross misunderstanding of solar energy. Solar cells and enormous batteries are very expensive and have a limited life span. Their practical applications are primarily limited to remote areas or on mobile applications where power from the grid is unavailable. For example, the author of this book needed electricity in a remote tool shed. This shed was too far from the house to conveniently run wire, so he installed solar power. After seven years of use, the cost of this solar power has averaged ten dollars per kilowatt-hour compared to ten cents per kilowatt-hour for the electricity coming into the house. It is true that the costs per kilowatt-hour would be reduced if this power were used more often. However, it is also true that the available solar power is limited, and a gasoline-powered generator was often needed in order to operate larger power tools.

Wind Power

> *For he commandeth, and raiseth the stormy wind, which lifteth up the waves thereof* (Ps. 107:25).

Another source converts the energy of the wind into electricity.

Wind energy fights many of the same limitations as solar energy. Although there is tremendous energy in the wind, windmills will always be inadequate in comparison to the energy available. Wind is also limited in that too little produces no power, and too much does not produce additional power. Furthermore, wind power is not constant. It is regional and seasonal. Therefore, for major utility applications, it must be stored. As is the case with solar power, this requires large highly inefficient batteries. Denmark is the forerunner in wind power. Their population pays *twice* what we pay in the United States for electricity even with government subsidies. On the other hand, in some cases wind power can be cost effective for individual home use. This is because the home would still have the power grid available to draw power from when the wind energy is low. This eliminates the need for the hefty power storage and substantially reduces the overall installation cost.

Geothermal Power

> *Bow thy heavens, O LORD, and come down: touch the mountains, and they shall smoke* (Ps. 144:5).

Geothermal power converts the heat in the earth into electricity. Although the available energy is enormous, the energy density is a function of the depth of the source. The deeper the source, the greater the geothermal energy, but the cost of drilling increases more rapidly with depth than the availability of the energy. Wind and solar energy are still far more cost effective than geothermal.

Nuclear Power

> *Wherein the heavens being on fire shall be dissolved, and the elements shall melt with fervent heat?* (2 Pet. 3:12).

Nuclear energy converts the energy released by splitting an atom into electricity. It is the second largest source of electric power in the United States. (Coal is the largest source of electric power.) This is a very controversial subject that far exceeds the scope of this text. The news media would have you equate the Chernobyl reactor disaster (April 26, 1986) to our Three Mile Island Reactor (TMI) accident (March 28, 1979) and the potential disasters pending at all of our other reactors. There is simply no similarity in the safety of Soviet era reactors designed by a society where life is expendable and the safety of U.S. reactors designed and built by a society that believes life is precious. The Chernobyl reactor had virtually no "containment vessel." The accident killed over 50 people as a result of direct short-term radiation exposure. Estimates of death due to long-term radiation vary wildly between 4,000 and over 90,000. U.S.-built reactors include a "containment vessel" (a structure around the reactor) to protect human life and the environment if a serious accident does occur. U.S. reactors also have multiple safety redundancies in the operation of the reactor. The Three Mile Island Reactor incident bares the fruit of that redundancy. The 1970 era computers safely and successfully shut the TMI reactor down even after multiple human attempts to bypass the safety features. The end result was minor melting within the reactor core (minor compared to a true "reactor melt down") rendering the reactor unfit for repair. However, this failure occurred without the loss of a single life.

From a "global warming" perspective, nuclear reactors emit no greenhouse gasses. From this respect, they are "green." However, although conventional nuclear power does not generate carbon dioxide and it is more cost effective than solar, wind, and geothermal power, it is not without significant setbacks. (Detonating like an atomic bomb is not one of them. This is not possible.) The first setback is the unknown cost of power plant construction. The last power plants built in the United States cost twice what they were originally estimated. This was not due to increased cost of construction materials or labor, but was entirely due to increased regulation and environmental court battles. It is difficult for a power company to justify a construction project with unknown costs. The second setback is the unknown laws that will dictate the handling of waste products. Companies have handled waste products fully in compliance with the laws at that time only to be faced with billion-dollar settlements decades later when the laws have changed. Power companies have no incentive to take that risk. It is worth noting that these first two "setbacks" are primarily "political" in nature, not technical. The third setback is not the radioactive waste of the reactors but the irresponsibility of the people and government facilities handling that waste. People still sin. That being the case, sin, emotional media, and hype — not technology — will almost certainly prevent any major comeback by the nuclear power industry here in the United States.

Gimmicks

Unfortunately, as the media and politicians continue to instill fear into society, we tend to fall prey to gimmicks that "sound" like logical solutions. This is particularly true in a period of rapid price increases. With today's rapid energy price increases, we need to be cautious about the promises that sound "too good to be true." They usually are just that. Generally, there is some unspoken price to be paid. The following chart will name just a few.

Gimmick	Claim	Unspoken Cost
Miracle carburetors	100 MPG or better on full size autos	This is merely an old myth.
Miracle gas additives	Significantly greater gas mileage	Improved gasoline specifications have virtually eliminated MPG enhancements by additives. Purchasing gasoline from reputable stations would be more effective.
Miracle engine oils	Significantly greater gas mileage.	Some synthetic engine oils do improve performance, but not spectacularly. Always check the vehicle's manufacturer's recommendations so as to not damage the engine or void the warranty.
BioFuels	Convert your local fast food fryer oil into fuel.	This may be useful for a few people willing to go to this effort, but it will not help with carbon emissions or with the energy crunch. Consider that one fast food restaurant produces enough waste to supply fuel for 2–3 people. Count the number of fast food restaurants in your town and compare that figure with the number of people in your town. It obviously would have little impact.
Cold Fusion	A revolutionary breakthrough has been made in fusion technology.	Although fusion ("fusing" two atoms together into one) may eventually become a viable source of energy, it is at least 50 years away and may never be viable.
Ocean Power — Harnessing the Tide	The tide is an enormous source of power	The tides are an enormous "example" of power; however, they are not a "source" because the power is spread out over such a large area. Mechanical costs would be prohibitively expensive.

Gimmick	Claim	Unspoken Cost
Ocean Power — Utilizing the Rankine Cycle	Large temperature gradients can provide power.	Most of the power available by this method would be used to pump the cold water to the surface and lost as the cold water warms during the process.
Three-wheeled autos	Due to their light weight, they obtain spectacular gas mileage.	Three-wheeled autos are not required to comply with federal safety standards. This is a major source of their ability to be lightweight.
Exhaust or engine emission modifications	Significantly greater gas mileage	Some modifications will increase the gas mileage, but they also increase undesirable emissions and are illegal.
Engine modification to run on water	The electricity from the alternator can generate hydrogen from water. The hydrogen can be burned as fuel.	This is total nonsense regardless of how many "testimonies" may be published. Hydrolysis of water (breaking it into hydrogen and oxygen) requires more energy than that which is produced by burning the hydrogen.
Solar-powered autos	No gasoline required	The vehicle will use power considerably faster than the solar cells can generate it, and it will not charge at night.
Hybrid autos	Spectacular gas mileage	It is possible to retrieve some lost energy from constant braking in continual stop and go city traffic. The "hybrid" technology has absolutely nothing to offer on the highway.
Compressed air autos	No gas, no emissions, fill up for free at any service station that has an air compressor.	To get any significant mileage on a single fill-up, the air is compressed to over 4,000 psi. The "free air" at a service station is only compressed to 100 psi. Once again, the emissions are all generated at the power plant that provided the energy to run the air compressor. Due to substantial heat generation, compressing air is very inefficient.

Gimmick	Claim	Unspoken Cost
Bicycles, mopeds, and motorcycles	Considerable gas savings	Be sure to consider traffic conditions, distance to travel, weather, travel time, and particularly safety. No gas savings will ever offset a broken neck.
"Solutions" already exist	They are being blocked by big business to protect their profits and investments.	We live in a competitive global economy. If a true "solution" did exist, companies would be racing to license it. Failure to embrace a solution would destroy the company.
"Work at home" opportunities	No more commuting	Productive telecommuting opportunities do exist, but does this opportunity actually provide income or just promises of income?

Some of the "gimmicks" above may actually suit your needs and be a viable means of saving money or caring for the environment. As good stewards of God's provisions, we need to always look for ways of being more responsible. Just be sure you embark on these ideas with your eyes fully open and recognize their true costs or limitations.

ANWAR

The debate over drilling in ANWAR has nothing to do with global warming but is certainly related to the energy crisis, so it

is worth mention- ing. ANWAR is an acronym for Arctic National Wildlife Refuge that includes ap- proximately eight million beautiful acres (or 12,500 square miles) and

Fairbanks

Anchorage

Arctic National Wildlife Refuge

0   200   400
Miles

A camp on the coastal plains of the Arctic National Wildlife Refuge with the Brooks Range in the background (U.S. Fish and Wildlife photo)

is about the size of South Carolina. It is east of Prudhoe Bay, the home of most of our arctic oil wells. According to the U.S. Fish and Wildlife Service, who provided the photo of the Brooks Range above, ANWAR is "a vast and beautiful wilderness, an intact continuum of six different ecological zones" and "was established to preserve unique wildlife, wilderness and recreational values; to conserve caribou herds, polar bears, grizzly bears, musk ox, dall sheep, wolves, wolverines, snow geese, peregrine falcons, other migratory birds, dolly varden, and grayling; to fulfill international treaty obligations; to provide opportunities for continued subsistence uses; and to ensure necessary water quality and quantity." It is often believed that drilling for oil in ANWAR will reduce our energy dependency on foreign oil. However, it should be noted that governmental drilling restrictions in general have caused our unprecedented dependency on foreign oil. The oil companies already have congressional approval to drill in areas west of Prudhoe Bay and have taken the next step of leasing the rights to this oil from the federal government, but have yet to pump any significant amounts of oil from those areas. The reason is strictly the cost of compliance with all the regulations. Once Congress approves drilling in ANWAR (if ever), we will still be many decades away from pumping oil from that area.

"Solution" Summary

We mentioned that the September 2004 issue of *National Geographic* dedicated 75 pages to global warming. After wading through the entire article, the very last page summed up the situation as follows: "Can we do anything to stop the change? No. . . . Even if we were to stop CO_2 emissions now, we are committed to warming."

That is not the only "change" that we will be unable to stop. We will not be able to stop the politicians from attempting to change our lifestyles. The future so-called solutions to global warming in the electric power arena will result in significantly increased costs of electric power. On the surface, you may be one of the few who consider the doubling or tripling of your electric bill to be palatable. However, increasing the price of electric power does not only affect your household electric bill. It affects the electric bills of every aspect of society. The price of every commodity in the country would increase dramatically, all for the sake of global warming hype. Remember, the costs of power generation are all borne by individuals, and not by some impersonal corporate entity. Since real "solutions" are mere phantoms, politicians are pressured to pass legislation, any legislation that gives the public the impression that they are conscientiously doing their job. This includes enacting lofty emission regulations with threats of hefty fines on corporations who have no practical means of complying. This form of regulation cripples our corporate infrastructure. Furthermore, legislation that cripples industry and our source of energy cripples us — you and me, the individual taxpayers.

Some of these "plans" require decades to implement and have price tags that would bankrupt even the healthiest economies. They are easy for legislators to pass when they know that they will be out of office (or dead) long before the real financial impact is felt.

This is a dire thought for a couple of reasons. Have you noticed that the legislation always has two contradictory, yet non-retractable, aspects? (a) We must end our dependency on foreign oil for political and economical reasons and (b) we must reduce or restrict our oil production at home due to environmental reasons. That is a bit of a dilemma! We cannot use foreign or domestic oil? The "global warming" issue is not just a national issue. As long as oil is available, nations will continue to use oil. Carbon dioxide will continue to be produced. These two seemingly contradictory "requirements" actually do serve a purpose, but that purpose has nothing to do with energy or the environment. It serves two very unfortunate purposes:

1. It truly does cripple healthy nations. This is the goal of socialist/communist ideology. Remember from our previous

discussions, the socialist/communist ideology falsely assumes that some nations are poor because others are rich. If they cripple the rich, the poor will have more.

2. It satisfies the need for political authoritarianism. We will discuss that point a little later in this chapter, but essentially, it satisfies one's sin nature for power.

This crippling effect hurts the rich and the poor, but certainly not equally. It may be true that in some cases a one-hundred-dollar cost for the rich is the same one-hundred-dollar cost for the poor, but the hundred dollars that we are talking about represents a significantly larger percentage of the working income of the poor than that of the rich. When the rich get hit with a higher heating bill, they can often afford it without batting an eye. On the other hand, the fixed or low-income families have no source for that extra cash. Effectively, this regulation becomes a terribly burdensome "tax" on the poor.

We would all agree that global poverty is considerably more destructive than global warming. People die as a result of poverty every day. According to some estimates, ten million children die every year as a direct result of poverty.[2] It is certainly true that the definition of "death due to poverty" is nebulous at best, but we can all agree that it is real. Yet, not one person has ever died due to the supposed half of a degree increase in global temperature. We can also all agree that energy will be required to help prevent and eradicate poverty. Energy is required to feed and clothe people. What will be the direct result of this global-warming hype? Increased energy costs, and therefore increased poverty. Once again, "The perfect crime is where the victim believes that he has been done a favor."

Consequently, these so-called solutions are really "poison pills." They are offered by politicians who have no real constructive platform and want to sound concerned for the planet. Their political platforms are merely a list of "anti-this" and "anti-thats" with no

2. www.Globalissues.org.

credible constructive solutions to anything. Unfortunately, these poison pill platforms are extremely effective. As you have noticed, the politics of the United States is becoming more polarized and split down the middle. Being able to articulate this poison-pill platform as effectively as possible can easily serve to swing just enough votes in either direction to win an election.

Enormous human energy is spent doing just that, articulating a precarious position as best as possible. But what are the actual effects of global warming, and does it really matter?

Effects of Global Warming

As shown earlier, it is difficult to quantify the global temperature increase due to increased carbon dioxide. However, experiments clearly show that increased carbon dioxide increases plant production! Increased plant life absorbs more water vapor from the atmosphere which will tend to cool the earth. Several studies have shown that increasing the carbon dioxide concentration from the current ambient of 0.03 percent to 0.05 percent causes an increased yield of 29 to 40 percent. Therefore, food production would actually increase significantly. Reducing the carbon dioxide in the atmosphere causes a proportionate decline in production. But these are not the effects that global warming alarmists would have us consider.

We have discussed automobiles because they are tools that personally and directly affect our daily lives. We have also discussed electric power, which affects our lives even more but seems to be less direct. In both cases, the so-called solutions to the supposed global warming problem have virtually no effect on the production of carbon dioxide. Yet they most certainly affect our expenses for daily living. The astute person would naturally ask, "How can this be? Why would scientists, our government, and the media constantly be pushing these solutions if they are totally counterproductive?" To answer this question, we must continually remind ourselves that the hype on global warming is emotional and political, *not* technical. We should also remember that the news media, movie stars, and rock bands are generally not technically inclined. Furthermore, referring to chapter 3, one considerable contributor to this hype is socialist/communist (anti-American) ideology. Yes, ideology, not honest merit. The socialist/communist advocates of global warming would like nothing more than to permanently cripple Western civilization.

What are the actual harmful environmental effects of a warmer planet? What if the temperature does increase another degree? Or even two degrees? This would be like moving south about two hundred miles. Is that doom and gloom? As the year 2005 came to a close, shortly after Hurricane Katrina and one of the worst hurricane seasons on record, the global-warming doomsayers were predicting that the next seasons would be even worse. There was considerable talk about minute changes in temperature causing enormous changes in hurricane intensity. The National Hurricane Center denied these allegations and came under instant political attack. But as Matthew 7:15 tells us, "Beware of false prophets." The 2006 hurricane season was one of the mildest ever. The 2007 hurricane season — just as mild as 2006! This has really frustrated the global-warming proponents. Little tropical storms get nearly

Hurricane
Fay

as much press as Katrina, just to fuel the fear frenzy. In 2008 the media hype became quite comical. "Hurricane Fay" was a classic example. The classic hurricane doom warnings were in your ear at every newsbreak:

> "FLORIDA RESIDENTS BRACE FOR DEADLY HURRICANE FAY," "FLORIDA RESIDENTS EVACUATE AS FAY THREATENS TO STRENGTHEN TO CATEGORY 3," "FAY MAKES ITS WAY TO THE THIRD LANDFALL IN FLORIDA," "AMERICAN RED CROSS AIDS FAY EVACUEES, PREPARES FOR GUSTAV."

Why is this so amusing? "Hurricane Fay" was never a "hurricane." She was only a "tropical storm."

Most scientists agree that a rising sea level is the greatest threat. This is extremely difficult to estimate, but it would *not* be 20 feet, as Al Gore has suggested. The IPCC has revised its estimates of increased sea levels in the year 2100 from three feet in the 2001 report to only 17 inches in the recent 2007 report. Another report published in the January 19, 2006, edition of *Nature Magazine* suggests that the sea level will rise only two inches by the year 2100. It is ironic that as scientists look deeper into this issue, the data and effects are diminishing as the hype is increasing.

Global Warming Political Propaganda

One of the most vocal advocates of pending doom due to global warming is Mr. Al Gore. A handout that accompanies his movie *An Inconvenient Truth* lists ten things that we can do to curb carbon dioxide emissions. Let's examine this list to objectively evaluate the results of these personal sacrifices. The right-hand column is the amount of carbon dioxide per year that would not be generated (according to Mr. Gore) if you followed his advice.

	Mr. Gore's Suggestion	Mr. Gore's Proposed Carbon Dioxide Savings, in Pounds per Year	My Assumption	Total Pounds per Year of Carbon Dioxide Savings
1	Change to fluorescent light bulbs	150 / bulb	10 bulbs	1,500
2	Drive less / carpool	1 / mile	2,500 mile savings	2,500
3	Recycle more	2,400	(none)	2,400
4	Check your tire air pressure	3 percent improvement in gas mileage	20 gallon savings	400
5	Use less hot water	850	(none)	850
6	Reduce your garbage by 10 percent	1,200	(none)	1,200
7	Adjust your thermostat by 2 degrees	2,000	(none)	2,000
8	Plant a tree	2,000 per life of tree	20 year life	100
9	Turn off electronic devices	"thousands"	This is rather nebulous! See note below.*	1,000
			Total =	11,950

*For this line item, Mr. Gore's savings was listed as "thousands of pounds." Hot water heaters use considerably more power than a computer, but we will use a figure of 1,000 pounds just to humor his illustration.

This brings the total carbon dioxide savings per year to a grand sum total of 11,950 pounds. Let's round this figure to 12,000 pounds, or 6 tons of carbon dioxide per year. That sounds like an enormous savings. Is it? The total amount of carbon dioxide in the atmosphere is over 3 trillion tons. A savings of 6 tons out of 3 trillion would not even be measurable.

Lastly, Mr. Gore says we need to tell others. (I suppose that was intended to be item #10.) Perhaps that is the key to his equation. Let's suppose you told others — a lot of others — and ten million households made the same sacrifices. Six tons per household times ten million households is 60 million tons of carbon dioxide. This sounds like an enormous savings until you consider that it represents less than 2 percent of the carbon dioxide in the atmosphere. According to the U.S. Geological Survey, volcanoes alone contribute more than twice that amount (130 million tons) per year into the atmosphere.

As we consider the future position of Christians in a world dominated by the global-warming hype, we can certainly say that there is nothing particularly wrong with voluntarily taking any of the above measures. As Christians, we are to be good stewards of God's provisions, but we must also ensure that we are not innocent victims of the perfect crime. We must notice that all of the items listed above cost time, personal energy, money, or personal comfort. It is a tragedy that some people have bought into this farce by making significant personal sacrifices with the expectation that they are doing their part to curb global warming when the results of their efforts cannot even be measured. They are being terribly and deliberately deceived. No apology is offered for the use of the word *deliberately*. Since Mr. Gore has the ability or resources to calculate the pounds of carbon dioxide savings for each of these items, he also has the ability or resources to calculate the overall benefits, which are immeasurable to insignificant.

But this is just "one man"; a politician, not a scientist. How do his numbers compare with those of the Environmental Protection Agency (EPA)? The following chart makes the comparison:

Mr. Gore's Suggestion	Mr. Gore's Proposed Carbon Dioxide Savings, in Pounds per Year	The EPA's Estimation of Savings
1 Change to fluorescent light bulbs	150 / bulb	100 / bulbs
2 Drive less / carpool	1 / mile	1 / mile
3 Recycle more	2,400	600
4 Check your tire air pressure	3 percent improvement in gas mileage	Not listed
5 Use less hot water	850	10 / kwh of use
6 Reduce your garbage by 10 percent	1,200	0 (This is included in #3 above)
7 Adjust your thermostat by 2 degrees	2,000	383
8 Plant a tree	2,000 per life of tree	23.2
9 Turn off electronic devices	"thousands"	10 / kwh of nonuse

You will notice that there are some substantial differences. Mr. Gore's combined savings evaluation for recycling and garbage is 3,600 compared to EPA's 600. Mr. Gore's two-degree thermostat change is 2,000 compared to EPS's 383. Just these two errors alone represent a loss of savings of over 4,600 pounds. That's almost 40 percent of his estimations! Once again, there is certainly nothing wrong with conservation and less waste, but if we are going to go to significant trouble and discomfort to do it, we need to understand that the effects will never be felt by the environment. The EPA calculation of savings using the Gore approach represents only 7,350 pounds of carbon dioxide, which corresponds to 0.0000001 percent of the carbon dioxide in the atmosphere. That's a lot of numbers and many people simply do not relate to numbers very well. Let's put this back into perspective. The proponents of global warming claim that you are responsible for this crisis. Yes, you are to blame. Yet if you do everything in your power to reduce the impact, you have only affected the overall concentration of carbon dioxide by a measly 0.0000001 percent.

Have you ever wondered how a politician has become so ridiculously popular on a scientific issue? What possible background does he have that makes him so successful in this arena? Be careful before you say, None. He has incredible credentials — those of politics, the powers of persuasion.

The concept of authority was established by God, and not by man. Ultimately, God makes the rules, not man. God's implementation of human authority was intended to be an extension of His authority. It is true that throughout history man has abused that principle. But we worship a sovereign God who works through sinners, including politicians. Herein lies the root of this political battle, though. Our nation was founded on principles of godly leadership. Our republic was intended to be led by numerous godly leaders. However, most of these numerous leaders have no desire to honor the Creator that established their authority. As a result, they believe that authority comes from them and not from God. If authority comes from them, they must wield it over others, as many others as possible. This is the root of totalitarianism. Fortunately, the United States does not have a totalitarian government, but it does have "totalitarian ideology" in various aspects of government. This ideological totalitarianism would like to punish all who disagree with their ideology. This can't really be true, can it? Absolutely. Legislation to punish those who produce carbon dioxide is on the table every day that Congress is in session. Fortunately, in the words of Joseph to his brothers, "But as for you, ye thought evil against me; but God meant it unto good, to bring to pass, as it is this day, to save much people alive" (Gen. 50:20). God's plan cannot be thwarted. He uses sinners on this earth to accomplish His purposes every day, and He can use evil legislation for His purpose as well.

The Greenhouse Effect

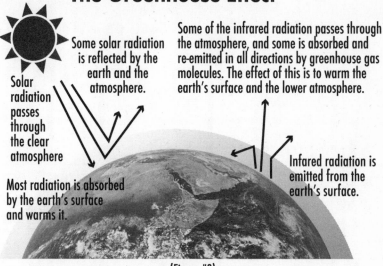

Some solar radiation is reflected by the earth and the atmosphere.

Solar radiation passes through the clear atmosphere

Most radiation is absorbed by the earth's surface and warms it.

Some of the infrared radiation passes through the atmosphere, and some is absorbed and re-emitted in all directions by greenhouse gas molecules. The effect of this is to warm the earth's surface and the lower atmosphere.

Infared radiation is emitted from the earth's surface.

(Figure #8)

Ask the Experts

The debate rages on. Or does it? One of the most effective ways to dodge a debate is to pretend that the debate is already over. This has been the primary "defense" of "evolution" for decades. We were told that former President Bush was "anti-science." Why was he labeled "anti-science"? Because when he first stepped into office on January 20, 2001, he did not blindly accept the "politically correct" consensus. He asked for time to review the data in order to make responsible policy recommendations. This was obviously not what the politically correct consensus wanted to hear. To them, the debate (that never began) was already over. Our Environmental Protection Agency (EPA) Web site uses this tactic very effectively. Naturally, if we want to find solid concrete evidence of global warming, we should ask the experts. In the United States, that would be the federal agency responsible for policing this type of environmental activity, the Environmental Protection Agency (EPA). Their climate change Web site, http://www.epa.gov/climatechange/, is massive! This one web page has 68 links that all link to countless others. It will quickly wear you out. The first question to "Ask the Experts" was, "Can you show

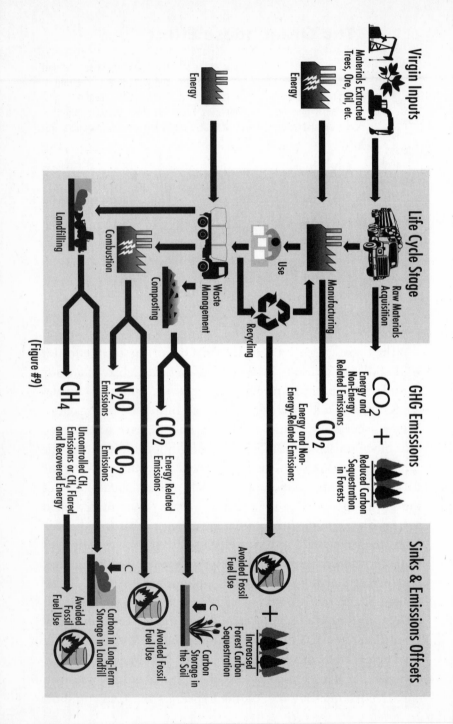

Virgin Inputs

Materials Extracted
Trees, Ore, Oil, etc.

Energy

Energy

Life Cycle Stage

Raw Materials
Acquisition

Manufacturing

Use

Recycling

Waste
Management

Composting

Combustion

Landfilling

GHG Emissions

CO_2 +
Energy and
Non-Energy
Related Emissions
Reduced Carbon
Sequestration
in Forests

CO_2
Energy and Non-
Energy-Related Emissions

CO_2
Energy Related
Emissions

N_2O CO_2
Emissions Emissions

CH_4
Uncontrolled CH_4
Emissions or CH_4 Flared
and Recovered Energy

Sinks & Emissions Offsets

Avoided Fossil
Fuel Use

+
Increased
Forest Carbon
Sequestration

Carbon
Storage in
the Soil

Avoided Fossil
Fuel Use

Carbon in Long-Term
Storage in Landfill

Avoided
Fossil
Fuel Use

(Figure #9)

me the raw data to support global warming?" Every link under SCIENCE was reviewed. A cute little cartoon entitled "The Greenhouse Effect" (figure # 9) was discovered, but it explains more about the absorption and reflection of energy from the sun than the greenhouse effect. The Web site includes enormous verbiage to define greenhouse gases, and how to reduce them. It includes one copyrighted temperature chart, but no raw data, and no explanations of how the data was gathered or how it was massaged to compensate for international non-standard temperature measurements. In short, the EPA Web site *assumes* that global warming is a reality and avoids any discussion to defend that position. Evidence to support the global-warming claims was conspicuously absent. Remember, extraordinary claims require extraordinary evidence to support such claims. The EPA Web site provides virtually no evidence, never mind *extraordinary* evidence.

Suppose you want to learn about what you can do about waste. You would expect the EPA Web site to clearly quantify the "specifics" of conservation. You click on WASTE and find a general page on the subject. You click on BASIC INFORMATION and find another general page. So you click on general information on the LINK BETWEEN SOLID WASTE AND GREENHOUSE GAS EMISSIONS and find another general page. Where are the specifics? On this page, you will find the statement, "The different sources of greenhouse gas emissions from waste are illustrated in the graphic to the right." The "graphic" is included on page 122 (figure #9). How this graphic describes the "Link Between Solid Waste and Greenhouse Gas Emissions" is difficult to tell. In this process, you will learn that "methane is a greenhouse gas 21 times more potent than carbon dioxide." But what are you to do about that? The Web site constantly refers to the term "solid waste reduction." But what exactly is "reduction"? Some solid waste can certainly be recycled. According to the EPA site, most recycling does save on carbon dioxide production, but no information has been provided on the cost effectiveness of doing so. Solid waste cannot be made to magically disappear (the first law of thermodynamics). We can change its state, we can use it again, we can place it in a landfill out of sight and out of mind, but we will never make it disappear. It will always be with us.

The subject of "methane" (also known as "natural gas") was an interesting one. According to the EPA Web site, 60 percent of the methane (which is a greenhouse gas 21 times more potent than carbon dioxide) in the atmosphere is "related to human-related activities." That is strange wording: "related to…"? Further analysis indicated that they included methane produced by food crops and livestock. All plants and animals (dead and alive) produce methane. If the crops and livestock were not growing in these areas, other plants and animals would be. Furthermore, scientists do not fully understand how living plants produce methane. As they continue to investigate methane production from living plants, they are realizing that they emit 10 to 1,000 times the amount of methane as dead organisms. This will have a significant impact on the estimated "man-made" methane.

There was one aspect of the Web site that was useful. As Christian stewards, we certainly do want to use our resources

responsibly. Under WHAT YOU CAN DO, the EPA Web site has a greenhouse gas emissions calculator. As responsible stewards, if we acknowledge that any reduction of greenhouse gasses  corresponds to a reduction in energy use, we can use this chart to help determine what lifestyle changes are more effective than others. As a humorous antidote, one recommendation was for you to mow your grass with a "mulching push mower." Not just any "push mower" (the cycle type with no engine) but a "mulching push mower" that makes it even harder to push. This suggestion was not included in the emissions calculator. If you were to use a push mower, you would probably exhale as much carbon dioxide as an engine-driven mower! Perhaps the solution to that ounce of carbon dioxide would be to cut the lawn with a pair of scissors.

The Kyoto Protocol

As we continue our look into the future, it is clear that industrialized countries will be pitted one against the other in a similar attempt to curb the so-called global warming by reducing greenhouse emissions. This is just what the world needs, another source of irritation between countries. This issue is becoming as polarized as communism. Since it is effective to prey on the conscience of individuals, it follows that it would also be effective to prey on the conscience of governments. The Kyoto Protocol, signed by many countries in December of 1997, is one such attempt. As you may recall, the United States did not sign that agreement. Was the United States anti-environmental? In this section, we will show that the United States was merely being honest and the countries that did sign on to the agreement have provided lip service only.

According to the International Energy Agency (IEA) the actual carbon dioxide production since 1990 has changed by:

Portugal	+59 percent
Spain	+46.9 percent
Ireland	+40.3 percent
Greece	+28.2 percent
Canada	+23.6 percent
Japan	+18.9 percent
USA	+16.7 percent
Netherlands	+13.2 percent
Italy	+8.3 percent
France	+6.9 percent
Britain	− 5.5 percent [3]
Germany	− 13.3 percent [2]

We should also note that no Third World countries have signed this agreement. According to Fatih Birol, the IEA's chief economist, this is an even greater problem. "We expect carbon dioxide emissions growth in China between now and 2030 will equal the growth of the United States, Canada, all of Europe, Japan, Australia, New Zealand, and Korea combined" (*Washington Post*, June 25, 2005). Why is China not pushed to agree to this protocol? At the end of the previous chapter, we discussed the various and differing reasons that so many people have bought into this global warming scheme. It is very difficult to determine the percentages of each group and their motives for agreement, but is it possible that the socialist/communist influence could be a considerable factor for the reason the socialist/communist countries have not been pushed to sign onto this agreement?

From the data above, it is clear that most countries that signed the Kyoto Protocol are considerably worse than the United States

---

3. British and German reductions are unrelated to the Kyoto agreement. Britain has been working for decades to eliminate their love affair with coal usage. Germany has been converting the old East German coal-fired power plants to much more cost-effective (and cleaner) facilities.

and have "failed" miserably. They have failed because there is little that man can do about it. It is also interesting to note that the numbers above do not take into account the size of the country. If we consider that the United States is considerably larger than any of these other countries, it places us in even better light. Using the U.S. Census Bureau data, the following chart converts this data into per capita increases.

Country	Percent Increase	Population	Increase / Million People
USA	+16.7 percent	299,297,748	+0.056 percent
France	+6.9 percent	61,021,469	+0.11 percent
Italy	+8.3 percent	57,986,304	+0.14 percent
Japan	+18.9 percent	127,417,000	+0.15 percent
Canada	+23.6 percent	33,002,658	+0.72 percent
Netherlands	+13.2 percent	16,472,905	+0.80 percent
Spain	+46.9 percent	40,341,000	+1.16 percent
Greece	+28.2 percent	10,668,000	+2.64 percent
Portugal	+59 percent	10,587,221	+5.57 percent
Ireland	+40.3 percent	4,064,395	+9.93 percent

Now the data is even more striking. If you listen to the media, the United States is the bad guy because it will not even sign on to the Kyoto Protocol, never mind actively pursue curbing any greenhouse gases. Yet when you look at the data on a per capita basis, the United States stands far above the rest of the world.

Have you ever heard that the United States leads the world in curtailing carbon dioxide emissions? According to the media, the United States is the single largest contributor to global warming. This media hype is not going to end any-time soon. Consequently, as we look into the future, the United States will be placed under continually increasing pressure to reduce emissions. As we have discussed above, these efforts will do little to reduce carbon dioxide emissions, if they do anything at all. But they will most certainly continue to increase your living expenses.

Economic Considerations

For many years, one of our largest economic fears was runaway inflation. In the early 1980s, inflation was so rampant that many companies could not even print price lists. The price of the commodity was determined at the time of delivery. Economic collapse was a strong possibility. Since then, our Federal Reserve has successfully curbed inflation by minor, albeit regular, adjustments in the prime rate. But what can the Federal Reserve do — or anyone else, for that matter — with runaway prices due to the pressures exerted by global-warming hype? These increased costs are real, not just inflationary, and will not be countered by inflationary incomes.

Over the years, big government has severely eroded our standard of living. We have justified most of those expenses because many support the needy and poor or they supposedly provide social benefits. In the case of global warming legislation, these restrictions will hit our poor and needy the hardest and will provide no social benefits. Since poverty can only be cured by energy and technology, global warming legislation will be the world's most insidious enemy to the war on poverty. Millions, if not billions, of people could die due to neglect in the name of "the war on global warming." These economic crippling effects will simply be costs with no benefits. As we consider global warming and God's plan, is this proper Christian stewardship? Is the "Good Samaritan" to price the poor out of existence? This is yet another example of the axiom, "The perfect crime is where the victim believes that he has been done a favor." These so-called solutions' will cost the "victims" (of which the poor will be hit the hardest) substantial time, money, and loss of lifestyle in the *false belief* that they are saving the environment.

Water Vapor

There is also one substantial irony/hypocrisy of this global warming hype. Have you been asked to stop breathing yet? You exhale considerably more water vapor than you inhale. Water vapor is also a greenhouse gas. However, it is never mentioned as such because it is absolutely vital to our atmosphere. (So is carbon dioxide.) Without water vapor, it never rains. Consequently, water vapor never enters into the discussion on global warming, yet it retains considerably more heat than carbon dioxide. Furthermore as carbon dioxide increases, plant life increases, which absorbs water vapor removing it from the atmosphere. This would tend to cool the earth. Let's examine the effects of water vapor compared to carbon dioxide.

Both gases absorb heat from sunlight and, therefore, potentially increase the earth's temperature. (Or so the theory goes. See chapter 3 for a more detailed discussion.) The concentration of carbon dioxide in the atmosphere is 0.055 percent by mass. The concentration of water vapor in the atmosphere is 1 percent. Consequently, there is *18.2* times more water vapor than carbon dioxide in the atmosphere. The specific heat of carbon dioxide is 0.82 joules/gram. The specific heat of water is 4.2 joules/gram. Consequently, each gram of water vapor holds *5.1* times as much heat as a gram of carbon dioxide of the same temperature. That being the case, the water vapor in our atmosphere is responsible for retaining 18.2 x 5.1 = 93 times as much heat as the carbon dioxide! We need to put that figure into perspective. Remember the carbon dioxide saving measures suggested by Mr. Gore? If ten million households could make a difference of 2 percent of the carbon dioxide, we must also consider that the actual effect on the total greenhouse effect would be 2 percent divided by 93, which is only 0.02 percent. (It would actually be even less. There are other greenhouse gasses that we have no control over and have not even considered.) That being the case, if *every* household in the United States achieved Mr. Gore's goals of reducing six tons of carbon dioxide per year, the net effect on greenhouse gases would be less than 0.2 percent per year.

At this point, the obvious global warming response would be, "Ah — so in 100 years, we could reduce the greenhouse effect by 20 percent!" (100 years times 0.2 percent per year.) Actually, this would be fallacious reasoning since we only have control over a small portion of the carbon dioxide in the atmosphere, and the greenhouse effects of water vapor are 93 times more than the carbon dioxide. But let's humor that argument for a moment.

No one considers that any efforts will be significantly noticeable in the next ten years. At best, global-warming crusaders anticipate that it could take a hundred years or more to resolve this issue. This extended time factor brings up two good points about the whole sham.

Perspective

First of all, the political aspects of this fiction (see chapter 4) are long lasting. They will outlast any candidate who intends to use it to win votes. Furthermore, the longer the time frame, the more urgent they feel the global warming battle cry can become. This can provide a powerful platform for any political candidate. He can easily raise intense fears about problems 20, 50, or 100 years away, knowing that he does not have to address them during his own term of office. His goal is simply to get elected. But his platform will only be as productive as the population is ill-informed. For this reason, our nation needs to grasp the principles of this book. This is the only way to derail this political charade.

Secondly, we need to understand the context of long periods of time. From an evolutionary time frame (see chapter 1), the logic is as follows: "If the earth has been around for billions of years, we must preserve it for billions of years." This is not possible – even without man-made influences. With time, the earth would die anyway due to a lack of tides to keep our bays and shores clean. (The tides are caused by the gravitational effects of the moon. In a few billion years, the moon's orbit and the earth's rotation would synchronize and eliminate the tidal forces. Then the dead bays and shores would poison the oceans.) Furthermore, suppose man has zero emissions and that global warming is limited to only natural entropy. If we use the NASA data from chapter 4, and extrapolate 0.005 degrees per decade for a mere 100,000 years (10,000 decades), the earth will be warmer by 50 degrees in a blink of an eye by evolutionary standards. Fortunately, we need not be concerned about the temperature of the earth 100,000 years from now. Our Creator has a better plan, which we will discuss in chapters 7 and 8.

Alternative Explanation

We have discussed the fact that credible long-term temperature data does not exist. When talking about long-term trends, the older data has too many uncertainties to compare with current data. We have also talked about the fact that the atmosphere is enormously stable and tends to self-correct for carbon dioxide concentrations. Furthermore, Mars and the Neptune moon, Triton, seem to be warming. This cannot possibly be a result of greenhouse gas production here on Earth. We have also established that the water vapor in the atmosphere holds 93 times more atmospheric heat than the carbon dioxide. With all of this information, let's suppose that the earth has been warming over the past couple of decades and ask the following question, "Is there an alternative explanation for this?" It turns out that there is. The sun is the earth's single largest energy source by far. Our sun's "solar activity" has an enormous effect on the earth's global temperature. Coral Ridge Ministries and Answers in Genesis produced a film called *Global Warming – A scientific and biblical exposé of climate change.* This documentary interviews numerous scientists with evidence to suggest that solar activity is the primary cause for the appearance of recent climate change.

The solar activity follows an unpredictable pattern with a rough average of 11 years per cycle. However, the solar activity appears to have fallen asleep and is long overdue. Solar hibernation (as it

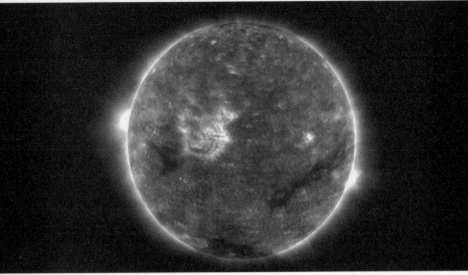

is called) happened in the 17th century and resulted in unusually warm weather followed by extremely frigid temperatures, resulting in crop death and famine throughout Northern Europe. (Northern Europe is not as accustomed to the cold as other northern geographic areas.) Some scientists of Canada's National Research Council are concerned that if the solar activity does not wake up in the next year or two, we could have a repeat of the late 17th century freeze! Due to crop damage, a "freeze" can be far more devastating than warmer weather.

Speaking of a "freeze," maybe we are still in an ice age and are simply pulling out of it. Well — that would explain the recent "warming" if this sign is correct (Natural History Museum of the Smithsonian Institute in Washington, D.C.).

Influence of Evolution Ideology

You may hear the term "sustainable environment." This is a very dangerous term. It does not mean sustainable for the next few decades or centuries. It means forever. This is not possible. The second law of thermodynamics dictates that the earth is winding down. It always has, and it always will. Environmentalists often blame man for this winding down. Effectively, if the environment changes by natural causes, it is considered to be simply part of the natural ecosystem, which is self-sustaining. On the other hand, if it can be linked to man, then the change is evil and unacceptable. For example, methane produced by livestock and crops is evil, but methane produced by wild animals and natural vegetation is perfectly normal! Similarly, population control via abortion and euthanasia is a perfectly acceptable means of achieving this goal of a sustainable environment. By their definition, the fewer people there are, the more sustainable the environment is.

The earth has not been here for billions of years. Nor is it going to remain here for billions of years. As discussed in chapter 4, it is not possible to determine if global warming is actually occurring due to carbon dioxide emissions. The fossil fuels that produce the carbon dioxide were all part of the ecosystem at one time in the past. The global plant life needs this carbon dioxide to survive. The ecosystem certainly appears to be self-regulating from a carbon dioxide frame of reference. On the other hand, as mentioned in the previous paragraph, the earth is winding down. This is a natural effect of the second law of thermodynamics. All energy functions are less than 100 percent efficient. The dissipated energy due to these inefficiencies is lost to the environment in the form of unrecoverable heat. This is truly global warming, but at a rate that is completely immeasurable and insignificant. Nevertheless, it is indicative of the second law of thermodynamics in general. Iron rusts to the point of being completely unsalvageable. Our landfills overflow with debris that is forever unusable. Ever since the Fall in Genesis 3, the earth has been winding down.

Biblical Perspective

This winding down is normal, but gradual global warming should not be alarming. Second Peter 3:7 states, "But the heavens and the earth, which are now, by the same word are *kept in store*, reserved unto fire against the day of judgment and perdition of ungodly men" (emphasis added). This verse reminds us that the earth is "kept in store" and is not going to perish due to gradual man-induced global warming. The world is being reserved until the Day of Judgment. What should be alarming is that, on that day, the globe will most certainly become very warm, but the warming will occur in a single day! "But the day of the Lord will come as a thief in the night; in the which the heavens shall pass away with a great noise, and the elements shall melt with fervent heat, *the earth also and the works that are therein shall be burned up*" (2 Pet. 3:10, emphasis added).

Chapter 6

Last Days - Scientific and Geopolitical

"We can solve tomorrow's problems with tomorrow's technology" (Al Gore).

As we begin our discussion of global warming and God's plan in the last days, we must first discuss "man's plan." In his politically correct environmentalist book *Earth in Balance*, and more recently in his movie entitled *An Inconvenient Truth*, the former vice president has entered into a biased pseudoscientific world of globalist government that is purported to solve the needs of this planet for peace and prosperity for the next millennium. These globalist environmentalists are totally ignorant of Scripture and science. They do not understand the influence of the evil one on mankind and the geopolitics of the world. They do not understand the science or the scientific data that paints a much more balanced picture of our environment.

Who are these "globalist environmentalists"? They come in all colors, sizes, and ideologies. Chapter 4 discussed "Ulterior Motives," which showed that people of all backgrounds have fallen for this hype. They may be political and ideological rivals on every front *except* for global warming. Many of these people are merely naïve and are going along with the agenda. However, far too many intend to drive government policy with this agenda.

These globalists, while often suppressing scientific data that does not support their cause, emphatically cite a whole list of issues in addition to global warming, such as famine, genocide, drugs, diseases, nuclear and biological threats, and environmental concerns as a reason for the establishment of a world government to take charge of these affairs, to solve the problems with modern science, and establish a millennium of peace. These people are willfully ignorant of the fallen nature of mankind, the evil in all religious systems that stand against the Gospel of Christ and nations that believe it. "Professing themselves to be wise, they became fools" (Rom. 1:22). With this in mind, this chapter will briefly try to bring the truth forth in the scientific and geopolitical scenarios of the present world.

A Scientific Look at the Uncertain Future

The Population Bomb

In 1968 the radical environmentalist Paul Ehrlich published the book *The Population Bomb*. This book panicked the world with dire predictions of millions dying of starvation. "The battle to feed humanity is over," he claimed. "In the 1970s and 1980s hundreds of millions of people will starve to death in spite of any crash programs embarked upon now." It fomented population control and forced abortions in some of the most populous nations such as China. Planned Parenthood and the UN have gone into the education and abortion battle armed with billions of dollars of propaganda, with the result that some are even talking now about a population implosion. Abortions worldwide are now being listed in eight figures with estimates ranging from 45 to around 60 million per year — 120,000 to 160,000! Even in light of these terrible statistics, there does remain a steady growth in the world population. These population control people could never convince the families of India to stop producing. In India, more workers in the family mean survival in their culturally induced poverty. Thus India will soon surpass China as the most populated nation in the world.

Historical records show that at the time of Christ the world population was approximately two hundred million, and reached one billion in A.D. 1800. Since 1930, the population of the world has tripled, going from two billion to six billion in the year 1999. It is projected to double again, meaning twelve billion people by the year 2015. These data are consistent with many written historical and scientific studies. It should be noted that these data going back to the year 2350 B.C. are entirely consistent with just eight souls surviving the flood epoch of Noah's day.

Water

The Ancient Mariner of the fabled rhyme said, "Water, water everywhere and not a drop to drink." The U.S. government study titled *Global 2000* predicted serious water shortages that would produce drought, famine, and conflict in various parts of the world by the year 2000. The crisis turned out to be not as acute as forecast, but it is still there and becoming more serious as *Global Trends 2015* predicts. Many of the water problems can be solved by technology, such as the desalination of sea water, deep wells with windmill pumps, and more, but it will be costly and there must be peace in the land to do the work.

Food

Both global studies 2000 and 2015 estimated food shortages would become critical with serious famine by the year 2015 in much of the so-called Third World. The United States and Canada can, with current production capability, feed a population of twelve billion (the projected population for the year 2015) with wheat, corn, and soybeans. The major deterrents to this happening are social injustice, political power struggles, and religious bigotry and restrictions. Two dreadfully striking examples of these problems were evident in 1970 when the United States sent several large ships full of grain to flood-ravaged Bangladesh and again in 2008 to Myanmar (Burma). The grain eventually rotted or was turned away unused while millions faced starvation.

Energy

Energy, which fuels the industrial nation's lifestyle, is abundant in the world in both replaceable and non-replaceable forms. The solutions to our energy needs are so tied up in the social and political struggles of fallen mankind that major conflicts are forecast. This very day we are arming certain countries in the Middle East to deal with other factions in the Middle East. So much of this has to do with the energy dependence of the developed countries of the Western Hemisphere and now China that it would be naïve to say that we can solve our needs without conflict in the form of war. There is abundant energy to meet the world's basic needs well into the next century. The known oil reserves (excluding shale oil) should last for 65 to 75 years. Coal reserves should last 150 to 250 years. Uranium reserves for nuclear power could last for many hundreds of years. Nuclear energy is the second largest source of electricity in the United States (second to coal). Unfortunately, due to the previous decades of media hype and fear mongers, no new reactors have been ordered

in the United States for over 30 years, and uranium mines will soon need major expansions. These projections are strictly for currently known reserves. Numerous other coal and oil fields exist that have not been mapped yet. However, with all this energy available, the use of this energy is unacceptable to many nations for a variety of reasons. For example, coal is an abundant source of energy that has been used for centuries, and could supply the free world's demand for the next century, but the environmentalists would like to remove it because it is said to produce smog, acid rain, and climate change, meaning — you guessed it — global warming.

Environment

There is little doubt that the environment is deteriorating. The needs of a burgeoning population make more and more water, energy, and land development demands on a post-Flood environment. As energy demands increase, the ubiquitous second law of thermodynamics ensures us that less and less energy will be available for use. Naturally occurring global warming has been going on since the first day of creation. To blame this on modern man and his machines does not hold true to the magnitude of the problem and the scientific evidence.

A Geopolitical Look at the Uncertain Future

The Free World – Secular Humanism and Naturalism

One of the best-organized attacks upon biblical revelation and morality is a tool of Satan called secular humanism. Consider the following statement by Richard Dawkins: "If you live in America, the chances are good that your next door neighbors believe the following: the Inventor of the laws of physics and Programmer of the DNA code decided to enter the uterus of a Jewish virgin, got himself born, then deliberately had himself tortured and executed because he couldn't think of a better way to forgive the theft of an apple, committed at the instigation of a talking snake." This is a direct quote from an advertisement for the *Free Inquiry* magazine, a publication of the Council for Secular Humanism. It is just one of many such blasphemous quotes in the war against God. This movement is promoted by many organizations. One such group, known as the American Humanist Association, has permeated our society with its *Humanist Manifesto I* (1933) and *Humanist Manifesto II* (1973). These documents, signed by a small number of influential people, hold significant power in many areas of society, and were an effort to throw God out of the areas of science, the arts, literature, education, the media, and government. The statement of *Manifesto II* that "No deity can save us, we must save ourselves," is the doctrinal pillar of this movement.

They are insisting that their so-called science (which is not science at all, but merely a consensus of political correctness) is the "truth" on which we must base our society. As opposed to religion, this system that permeates our educational institutions is at war with God and the faith-based, historically accurate worldview of Christianity. As Ben Stein so clearly demonstrated in his documentary *Expelled*, dissenters from their circle of influence are singled out and politically executed.

Islamic World

The Islamic world is polarized against Israel and the United States. All the implications of this situation are really best described in Dr. Curtis's book *The Last Days of the Longest War*, which we previously discussed. Suffice it to say that the biblical scenario of the end times for this earth seems to fit the situation of the rise of Islam in these days.

Communistic World

The atheistic/communistic world likewise is still large in the world picture with such nations as Russia and China set to play a dominant role (again) in the last days. The restrictions on real-time media coverage at the 2008 Olympics in China should be a wake-up call to those who feel that communism and mind control have perished.

Hindu World

The Hindu world of India, which will soon be the most populated nation in the world, was just mentioned because it is so large and is opposed to Christianity, even to the point of murdering Christians in India. In summary, by examining the world populations, science, our environment, and the geopolitical arenas, with or without global warming, the future certainly does not appear to be rosy. Furthermore, when we consider what man can actually do to resolve these situations, the results are depressing to grim. As a Christian, how are we to respond to these threats? Fortunately, God has a plan for our future. The plan does not include this fallen world.

Chapter 7

Millennial Age with the Return of Christ

The Millennial Kingdom
(see Isa. 11:1-16; 65:18-25, Rev. 20:1-10)

Purpose of the Millennial Kingdom

The purpose of the millennial kingdom is the establishment of a theocratic kingdom centered in Israel, whom God calls His Glory. God's relation to Israel is permanent (see Deut. 4:37, 7:8), as Moses said to God, recalling the promises given in Genesis:

> *"Remember Abraham, Isaac, and Israel, Your servants, to whom You swore by Your own self, and said to them, 'I will*

multiply your descendants as the stars of heaven; and all this
land that I have spoken of I give to your descendants, and they
shall inherit it forever'" (Exod. 32:13; NKJV).

Thus we look for God to restore the land to Israel in the last days. This will be a restoration where Jesus the Messiah will reign in Jerusalem (see Ezek. 34; Zech. 14; Matt. 24; Rev. 20), fulfilling God's promises to Abraham, Israel, and David (see Isa. 24:23). Furthermore, the millennial age marks a return to Genesis 1, where God gave man the rule over the earth, which man deeded over to Satan at the Fall. This is clearly understood when we read that Satan offered Jesus the rule that Satan said had been delivered to him (see Luke 4:6). But the second Adam, Jesus, defeated Satan at the Cross, and He will rightfully rule this kingdom (see Rom. 5; Rev. 20).

This millennial kingdom is a time when Satan is bound. Yet mankind — the portion who are still in the flesh — will still have to choose whether to be a child of the King. This kingdom is centered in Jerusalem with Jesus the Messiah ruling in David's seat with the faithful of Israel, while the faithful believers of the time from Adam to Abraham and the Gentile church are spread throughout the world administering the kingdom as resurrected saints. It is the ultimate fulfillment of all the Old and New Testament promises for a kingdom to Israel, as expected by the Apostles (see Acts 1:6). Just exactly what the saints will be doing as they live and reign with Christ can only be guessed at (see Rev. 20:6).

John understood that the nation of Israel would have the priestly role to be administering the offerings and worship (see Isa. 61:6; Zech. 8:20–23; Exod. 19:6), as well as controlling access to Christ and His judgments. Certainly there will be many administrative responsibilities that will be given to the saints, as the people of the world will work and worship in the seventh millennium. Life span may be extended back to the pre-Flood levels with many living as long as 900 years (see Gen. 4–5; Isa. 5:18–25). This time,

God will constitute a theocracy where Jesus, the last Adam, will reign with His saints (see Rom. 5:12–21; Rev. 20:1–10).

Physical Conditions in the Millennium

The passages in Isaiah chapters 11, 35, 51:3, and 65:20–25 all denote some reordering of the natural world. This could possibly include a reversing of current undesirable environmental and inefficient food and energy distribution problems and possibly even a return to the Edenic state of Genesis chapter 1 as mentioned previously (see Matt. 19:28). This "reversal" can only be possible by divine intervention. This should not sound so astounding. It is our Creator who maintains the physical laws (Jer. 33: 25–26; Col. 1:17; and 2 Pet. 3:7). Therefore, it is our Creator who can suspend these laws for the outworking of His plan. As described in previous chapters, man is incapable of solving these problems. The configuration of the nation Israel at this time is described by Ezekiel as he lays out the land and the city with its millennial temple where the Messiah will be enthroned (see Ezek. 40–47). There are some interesting passages that relate to the environment and ecology in Isaiah and Ezekiel. Isaiah 11 speaks of an animal kingdom without fear and predation, which may be entirely consistent with Ezekiel 47:1, which speaks of an Edenic time when mankind returns to being fruit-eating vegetarians.

But this is not the new heaven and new earth of the eternal state that is covered in the following section. It will be a joyous time when "the ransomed of the LORD shall return, and come to Zion with songs and everlasting joy upon their heads: they shall obtain joy and gladness, and sorrow and sighing shall flee away" (Isa. 35:10). This millennial kingdom is also part of the redemptive work of God. It is the answer to our prayer that Jesus taught us to say: "Thy kingdom come. Thy will be done, as in heaven, so in earth" (Luke 11:2). It will also be a fulfillment of the many prophecies relating to a restored Israel with David's seed on the throne.

Inhabitants of the Millennial Kingdom

Resurrected: Old Testament Saints (see Dan. 12:2, 13), and New Testament Saints (see 1 Thess. 4:17–19; 2 Tim. 2:12; Rev. 7; 20:3–4). These saints are reigning over the millennial kingdom with Jesus the Christ, David's seed, as King in Jerusalem (see Rev. 20:6). Every ruler is a resurrected saint and will be perfect in judgment and justice as they are now sinless and immortal.

Living Remnant of the Tribulation: A saved remnant of the Jews, and a certain number of Gentiles (see Zech. 12–14; Jer. 30:19–20; Ezek. 47:22). These Gentiles are apparently the participants in the final rebellion or the last war after the millennial age when Satan is loosed for a little while (see Rev. 20:7).

Time Period

This period will last 1,000 years (see Rev. 20:1–10), immediately following the great tribulation (see Rev. 4–19). This would perfectly fulfill the teaching of the Talmud that there was to be a period of six millennia of man followed by one millennium of rule by the Messiah.

The Great White Throne (Rev. 20:11-15)

After the completion of the seventh millennium of man, the final rebellion of mankind occurs as Satan is released to claim his last subjects for his infernal kingdom. This group is made up of those who would not accept Jesus as Lord in the millennial age. The participants in this final rebellion are probably most tied to Ezekiel 38–39 and the nations of Gog and Magog (see Rev. 20:8; Ezek. 38:2, 39:1, 6), which represent those who dwelt on the earth during the millennial kingdom and never came up to Jerusalem to pay homage to Christ (see Zech. 14). This final rebellion is defeated and the final judgment is begun. People are judged according to their works, which implies levels of punishment in the lake of fire for all who did not obey the gospel of Christ (see 2 Thess. 1:8).

The Scripture in several places indicates levels of punishment, as Jesus Himself said in Matthew 23:14. It should be noted that there is also a judgment of believers, although not at the great white throne event, since this is a judgment separating the people who are not in the Lamb's Book of Life. The judgment of believers most likely takes place at a prior time (see 2 Cor. 5:10), prior to the assignment of ruling positions in the kingdom with levels of rewards and position for those who are in the Lamb's Book of Life (see Rev. 20:15; 1 Cor. 3:11–15). It is conceivable that it is at the end of all judgments that the prophecy of 2 Peter 3:10 will be fulfilled, bringing an end to this fallen and condemned world, thereby paving the way for the new heavens and earth that are to follow.

Cha

Ne⋯ ⋯ and New Earth

And I John saw the holy city, new Jerusalem, coming down from God out of heaven, prepared as a bride adorned for her husband (Rev. 21:2).

Here is a picture of the New Jerusalem as described in the text:

A 1,500-mile, square-based pyramid shining like a glass diamond with a river running out of the throne at the apex. The river winds down through the holy city with trees along each bank, then out upon the earth that sits under the city. (See Rev. 21 and 22.)

The New Jerusalem, the Eternal City

From a secular point of view, when we look into the future,

there appears to be a time when the dimming lights appear to go out. The unbeliever, with his lack of faith, has no hope for the future. "Now faith is the substance of things hoped for, the evidence of things not seen" (Heb. 11:1). Our Creator has not left us in the dark regarding the final question that every man asks in this life, "What is my hope after death?" The Bible is full of God's promises of eternal life. Most notable is the promise Jesus gave us on the night before He was crucified when He said: "In my Father's house are many mansions: if it were not so, I would have told you. I go to prepare a place for you" (John 14:2). It is evident that if eternal life, which is promised to all who believe on the Lord Jesus the Christ (see John 3:16), and this place are to be all that they should be, the New Jerusalem must be in an environment that is radically better than our present one. In short, we need a whole new creation, that is to say a new heaven and a new earth. This is precisely what God has promised in His message to the apostle John as recorded in Revelation 21–22. This is the city that all of God's seed have looked for from the time of Genesis on to the present. Hebrews 11:10 states that the Old Testament believers "looked for a city which hath foundations, whose builder and maker is God." This did not change with the appearing of God's Son on this sin-cursed planet, as Hebrews again states. "For here have we no continuing city, but we seek one to come" (Heb. 13:14).

Let us study our way through these two chapters. The apostle John writes:

> *And I saw a new heaven and a new earth: for the first heaven and the first earth were passed away; and there was no more sea. And I John saw the holy city, new Jerusalem, coming down from God out of heaven, prepared as a bride adorned for her husband. And I heard a great voice out of heaven saying, Behold, the tabernacle of God is with men, and he will dwell with them, and they shall be his people, and God himself shall be with them, and be their God. And God shall wipe away all tears from their eyes; and there shall be no more death, neither*

sorrow, nor crying, neither shall there be any more pain; for the former things are passed away (Rev. 21:1–4).

Thus we see our Creator's plan; this new heaven and earth that is to be governed from a city called the Holy City, new Jerusalem. The new creation differs from the present as follows: no more sea (21:1), no more tears (21:4), no more death (21:4), and no more sorrow, crying, or pain (21:4). It should be noted that with no more sea there is still a river coming out of the throne (22:1). This river runs down and out all over the earth to provide water to the trees and wherever else it is needed.

The promise of blessing and the contrast of that which is outside the city is emphatic in Revelation 21:5–8. John writes:

> *And he that sat upon the throne said, Behold, I make all things new. And he said unto me, Write: for these words are true and faithful. And he said unto me, It is done. I am Alpha and Omega, the beginning and the end. I will give unto him that is athirst of the fountain of the water of life freely. He that overcometh shall inherit all things; and I will be his God, and he shall be my son. But the fearful, and unbelieving, and the abominable, and murderers, and whoremongers, and sorcerers, and idolaters, and all liars, shall have their part in the lake which burneth with fire and brimstone: which is the second death.*

This last verse (8), along with 22:11, clearly marks this as the eternal condition, and there is now no change possible for those who passed through the previous dispensations without putting their faith in the Christ.

Revelation 21:9–22:5 delineates the physical features of the city. John writes:

> *And there came unto me one of the seven angels which had the seven vials full of the seven last plagues, and talked with me, saying, Come hither, I will shew thee the bride, the Lamb's wife. And he carried me away in the spirit to a great*

and high mountain, and shewed me that great city, the holy Jerusalem, descending out of heaven from God, having the glory of God: and her light was like unto a stone most precious, even like a jasper stone, clear as crystal (Rev. 21:9–11).

Two important points are made here. First of all, this is the city whose builder and maker is the God that all the believers of Hebrews chapter 11 have looked for from the time of Abel. Second, the word translated *light* in verse 11 means a *brilliant* light. This place glows like the sun.

Revelation 21:12–21 describes a real city with walls, gates, dimensions, and materials. Verses 12–14 state:

> *And had a wall great and high, and had twelve gates, and at the gates twelve angels, and names written thereon, which are the names of the twelve tribes of the children of Israel: on the east three gates; on the north three gates; on the south three gates; and on the west three gates. And the wall of the city had twelve foundations, and in them the names of the twelve apostles of the Lamb.*

These verses show the true relation of the leaders of the faithful both before Christ's advent and after. The word that is translated *foundations* implies that this city rests on the earth and is not suspended in the air. Verses 15–17 give some clear dimensions as John writes:

> *And he that talked with me had a golden reed to measure the city, and the gates thereof, and the wall thereof. And the city lieth foursquare, and the length is as large as the breadth; and he measured the city with the reed, twelve thousand furlongs. The length and the breadth and height of it are equal. And he measured the wall thereof, an hundred and forty and four cubits, according to the measure of a man, that is, of the angel [apparently men and angels will be the same size in eternity as we are now].*

The Greek word translated *furlong* in the English is the length of a Greek Olympic stadium, and the 12,000 furlongs converts to a distance of roughly 1,500 statute miles. The square base from the Greek word *tetragonos* only applies to the base. This word describes a polygon, which is two-dimensional (e.g., pentagon, hexagon, octagon are all polygons) not a polyhedron, which is three-dimensional. If the writer John were describing the whole city, meaning anything but the base floor plan, he would not have used this word.

The wall is only 144 cubits (the length of a man's forearm and extended fingers), so the wall is only 216 feet high. Thus the statement that the height of the city is also 1,500 miles probably means that the city is a pyramid. This makes sense when we see the river proceeding from the throne (see Rev. 22:1), and the throne at the apex of the city, which may be what Ezekiel saw. This would also be God's answer to the concept of man at Babel and afterward around the world that the building of pyramids/ziggurats was an object of the divine configuration in which to dwell. It also explains God's comment and judgment at Babel. Consider, if the people understood that God would build a city that was promised to look like the tower, and that He would dwell there with His people, and now Nimrod builds this city and puts himself in the place of God, we can now understand God's statement that the people were trying to make a name for themselves and take on the aspirations to be as God (see Gen. 11:1–9), which is the same thing Satan imagined as discussed in chapter 3.

The materials seen in verses 18–21 are not only seen as precious and pure. Both Philo and Josephus see in them a correspondence to both the jewels on the high priest's garment and the signs of the Zodiac, which was originally given, not as satanic astrology, but as the gospel in the stars. This subject was covered in the book entitled *Specific Revelation: The Gospel Prior to Moses*[1] by William Curtis. John records in Revelation 21:18–20:

> And the building of the wall of it was jasper: and the city was pure gold, like unto clear glass. And the foundations of the wall of the city were garnished with all manner of precious stones. The first foundation was jasper; the second, sapphire; the third, chalcedony; the fourth, an emerald; the fifth, sardonyx; the sixth, sardius; the seventh, chrysolite; the eighth, beryl; the ninth, a topaz; the tenth, a chrysoprases; the eleventh, a jacinth; the twelfth, an amethyst.

Revelation 22:1 sees a pure river of living water. This is a common thought in this passage (21:6; 22:17; see also John 4:14 and 7:38). This river is clear as crystal, proceeding from the throne of God and of the Lamb. The oneness of God and His Son the Lamb are seen here, and there is but one throne (22:3), as seen in Colossians 2:9, Hebrews 1:3, and 1 Corinthians 15:28 (a verse with eternal relationship in mind).

Revelation 22:2 sees this river, flowing down throughout the city, as being lined with trees that bear 12 fruits, each yielding its fruit every month. This implies a new calendar with an eternal progression of events. This implies that we will go on in the eternal city with events and things to do as we live and reign with the Creator. It appears from Revelation 21:24–7 that the city will be open to the nations of those who are saved (v. 24), and we will come and go in administering the honoring of God throughout the earth. The new earth thus will have a capital — the new Jerusalem that God created for His people (21:2–3) — from which

---

1. William, Curtis, *Specific Revelation: The Gospel Prior to Moses* (Columbus, GA: Brentwood Christian Press, 1993).

all the earth is administered by God and His children. The new earth is apparently divided into nations (21:24) who bring their glory and honor to Jerusalem and receive the healing fruit (22:2). There is a tie here with Ezekiel, who saw the river flowing out of Jerusalem into the world with an ever-widening influence and with trees along the banks, as well as the idea of healing being provided (see Ezek. 47:1–12).

There will be no night in the new Jerusalem (v. 25), or any sun or moon in the new system (v. 23). It is also clear that this entire scenario is based on the Genesis record as literal history since the statement is made that the Curse of Genesis 3 is ended (see Rev. 22:3). There is pure water in the river of life proceeding out of the throne, and trees of life that provide 12 kinds of fruit. These trees, which take us all the way back to Genesis 3, will be reconstituted in the eternal city (see Rev. 22:2). There will be no night because eternal light is provided by the Creator. Neither will we need rest, and therefore there will be no lamp or sun (see Rev. 22:5). We whose names are written in the Book of Life (21: 27) will be servants of God (22:3). It is clear that in this eternal kingdom we will have work to do in service to the Lord. Our assignments will be commensurate with our faithfulness in this life, as Jesus points out in this same revelation, stating: "My reward is with me, to give every man according as his work shall be" (Rev. 22:12). The Scripture goes on to say that we will see His face (22:4), and reign forever and ever (22:5).

This is the best place promised to all who believe (see John 14:1–6). Inside this beautiful city, which is 1,500 miles square at the base and 1,500 miles high to the peak (21:16), are all the godly seed (see Rev. 22:14). While this city is enormous, capable of housing 40 billion people of our present physical size, it is not unlimited in size. This tells us that there is a limit to the size of God's family, and hence a limit to the ongoing creation of souls on this earth, and a time limit for such. In short, the seven–millennium period for this process makes some sense, which is another reason to believe the Genesis timeline. This thought should also spur those who believe that we are in a race to spread the gospel, an analogy that the apostle Paul used repeatedly (see 1 Cor. 9:24; 2 Tim. 4:7; Heb. 12:1).

This eternal city is not one made with hands, but is one that came down out of heaven made by God (see John 14:1–3; Heb. 11:10; Rev. 21 and 22). The new Jerusalem is indeed all we could hope for and need as we live in the eternal presence of our Creator according to His plan. It is a miraculous hope for mankind, the real purpose of God in our creation.

Chapter 9

Conclusions

And I saw a new heaven and a new earth; for the first heaven and the first earth were passed away; and there was no more sea (Rev. 21:1).

God's Promise

At this point, you may be wondering, *What does the millennial kingdom and the new earth have to do with global warming?* In an era where the media and politicians are preaching doom, gloom, and panic, we need to be clearly reminded that God has a plan for the future and has provided us with clear promises for the things to come! God's promise of a new earth overrides any need for man to save this present earth through draconian efforts that, in the final analysis, will not work. Back to our question at the end of chapter 6, "As Christians, how are we to respond to these threats?" We are to do what is right in the eyes of our Lord. In the context of this discussion, we are to do what we were always intended to do, "to be good stewards." Being good stewards does include minimizing waste and using our resources responsibly. According to the 2000 EPA Annual Report, between 1970 and 1999 the total emissions of the six principal air pollutants decreased by 31 percent. This is, of course, a good thing (which is why we seldom hear about this in the news media). These pollutants declined during a period of population growth, increased production, and significantly increased automobile mileage. However, if we swallow the "bait" of global warming political correctness, we will find ourselves wasting valuable money (on gimmicks and other "false solutions"), food (to burn as fuel), time (making lifestyle changes with little to no effect), and human energy (worrying or feeling guilty about something over which you have no control). This would *not* be good stewardship. But even more importantly, we must not lose sight of our ultimate purpose here on earth, to serve and honor Him. "Thou shalt love the Lord thy God with all thy heart, and with all thy soul, and with all thy mind" (Matt. 22:37). You do what is right in the eyes of the Lord, and He will take care of the details.

This present earth is under the curse recorded in Genesis 3. This curse was geological, meteorological, and botanical, as discussed previously. From chapter 1 through chapter 6 we have presented the history of this present earth. The physical, environmental, and geopolitical conditions of the earth foreseen for the year 2015 should convince our governments, which are dominated by Christian and Jewish ideals, that any such harsh effort to save the planet in its present cursed condition is not only futile but a false hope not given by the Creator of life and earth. Chapters 7 and 8 have presented the ages to come based on His promises. Beyond the final declaration of the present earth's passing, there are more passages in Scripture that declare that the earth is perishing. Psalm

102:25–27 clearly foresees the earth and heavens "waxing old like a garment" and then being changed. This passage is quoted by the writer of the Book of Hebrews. The text articulates the second law of thermodynamics or law of entropy, indicating that everything in the physical universe is growing old and wearing out. God created everything in the beginning and it was good. Then sin entered and the Curse has had the world running down ever since. Jesus said that heaven and earth are passing away (see Matt. 24:35). This universal scientific law of entropy is also spoken of by Isaiah: "The earth shall wax old like a garment, and they that dwell therein shall die in like manner" (Isa. 51:6). The law of decay and death applies both to the earth and its inhabitants. This clearly refutes the concept of evolution. The apostle Peter in chapter 3 of his second letter not only refutes the teaching of evolution that says "the present is key to the past," but he also reminds the scoffers by this world has been judged at the Flood and markedly changed. He also distinctly declares that this present system is going to be changed one last time. Peter writes, "The heavens being on fire shall be dissolved, and the elements shall melt with fervent heat. . . . Nevertheless we, according to His promise, look for new heavens and a new earth, wherein dwelleth righteousness" (2 Pet. 3:12–13). Global warming, that is, a slow warming, is not pictured by Peter. This reference to the heavens being on fire is initiated by a *megaphone* (3:10) in the Greek text. That's right, a big bang.

Closing Scientific Statements

Numerous scientific studies are being published that deny the Al Gore approach to so-called global warming. A few citations should be of interest to the reader.

Both the Institute for Creation Research and Answers in Genesis Web sites contain technically reviewed papers by nationally accredited scientists, which give a sound perspective on the global warming picture.

Professor emeritus William Gray of the Department of Atmospheric Science at Colorado State University as well as a research fellow at the Independent Institute, which issues the Atlantic Basin hurricane forecasts, has released a paper showing that there is no connection between global warming and the weather patterns in the Atlantic Basin. Over the past 150 years, there has been a slight increase in major hurricanes. Professor Gray has documented that carbon dioxide is not the cause nor has the temperature rise of half a degree Celsius been a factor. It was shown that in the periods studied from 1900 to the present, the hurricanes have both increased and waned with little or no change in carbon dioxide. It has also been shown that while the temperature increased half a degree and the carbon dioxide increased 20 percent in the period spanning 1925–1965, the number of hurricanes hitting the United States declined.

Meteorologist Augie Auer of New Zealand, writing in the May 2007 *Timaru Herald*, states, "Man's contribution to the greenhouse gases is so small that we couldn't change the climate if we tried, and water vapor is responsible for 95 percent of the greenhouse effect. Carbon dioxide (CO_2) is responsible for 3.6 percent of the greenhouse effect and man's activities only 3.2 percent of that, meaning only 0.1 percent of the greenhouse effect results from man's activities."

It is easy to find scientists to support views on either side of the debate. "Consensus" is never a problem. However, "consensus" has nothing to do with whether or not something is true. One of the most disturbing aspects about "politically correct" science, whether it is creation/evolution or global warming, is the notion that "there is consensus on this issue, therefore it must be true." This is absurd. For one reason, there is "consensus" on both sides of the issue. Contradictory sides cannot both be true. The "politically correct" consensus is simply the one determined by the news media and politicians and is therefore the one you hear the most often. That does not mean that it is necessarily correct. If "consensus" was the determining factor to determine truth, then:

- The world was flat at one time. Now it is a sphere.

- Life spontaneously generates from non-life. Now it doesn't.

- The only true god (consensus of one geographic area) is Allah. The only true god (consensus of another geographic area) is Buddha. *And* (not "or") the only true God is the triune Father, Son, and Holy Spirit. By definition (consensus) all three of these statements must be true simultaneously.

Obviously, this is nonsense. "Consensus" does not establish truth.

A book of this nature often has 20 pages of references in the back. However, the purpose of this book is not to solicit "scientific consensus." The purpose is to articulate the most accurate information as is humanly possible using the sound biblical and scientific principles that the Lord has so graciously (and patiently) provided. Many references are included in the body of this text, and many more could be added if the authors were concerned about an appearance of "consensus." Although it is technically correct to include as many references as possible with technical papers, even this often becomes merely a means to mask the truth with "consensus." Quite often, authors have never even read their technical references; they just reference as many papers as possible that appear to support their cause. Also, quite often, authors reference other papers without any effort to determine the validity of that position or data. Unfortunately, too much of so-called science has become nothing more than a "popularity contest." How sad.

The peer review process is broken beyond repair. Technical input contrary to the agenda of the author is completely disregarded. Consider the "peer reviewed" guidelines for environmental site investigations as published by the EPA. (http://www.epa.gov/swerust1/pubs/esa-ch0.pdf) According to this document, Jay Auxt was one of "the most significant contributors to the technical review process" yet the glaring flaws that he and other reviewers revealed during the review process of this document were completely ignored. What value is a "peer review" when that review is completely disregarded?

So how are we to process all of this information? We have mounds of hype built on top of mounds of hype. We have considerably more hype to process than actual data. This is not to suggest that data does not exist, it's just that we keep being presented with "selective data." How are we to formulate any reasonable, rational conclusions? To address this question, let's break it down into five questions:

Question 1: Is the world getting warmer?

Answer 1: We do not know. The amount of energy that is received by the sun and reflected back into space far exceeds and dominates the equations so dramatically that all of these other arguments and data banks pale in comparison.

Question 2: Doesn't the second law of thermodynamics provide energy from natural causes in the form of heat and entropy that tends to "warm" the earth?

Answer 2: Yes. This has been the case since the beginning of time.

Question 3: Since man uses energy and this energy can never be fully recycled (also the second law of thermodynamics), doesn't this tend to produce more man-made energy in the form of heat and entropy that tends to "warm" the earth?

Answer 3: Yes. This has also always been the case.

Question 4: Since the industrial revolution, isn't man using considerably more energy than ever before and thus producing even more energy in the form of heat and entropy that tends to "warm" the earth?

Answer 4: Yes.

Question 5: Is this something we need to be alarmed about?

Answer 5: No.

We do not need to be alarmed about this for five reasons.

Reason 1: As discussed previously, our Creator has a plan for this earth just as He has a plan for your life. God can use weather, celestial beings, and, yes, even you to fulfill that purpose.

Reason 2: God designed this earth in a most spectacular manner. When you cut your finger, it heals. God designed you that way. God also designed the earth with tremendous healing properties as well. Any planet that can survive a worldwide flood can heal from practically anything.

Reason 3: The data does not support an alarmist viewpoint. Selective data does support an alarmist view. Other selective data squarely disputes that view.

Reason 4: Even if the world is in a worst-case runaway warming scenario, there is nothing mere man can do about it. Man truly only has control over a small fraction of man-made greenhouse gases. Most are *required* for survival, and they cannot be stopped without other considerably more dire consequences.

Reason 5: God has a plan for your life that far exceeds worrying about whether He has control of the weather. "Are not two sparrows sold for a farthing? and one of them shall not fall on the ground without your Father" (Matt. 10:29). Engaging in these arguments for the sake of arguing will serve no useful purpose. The Scriptures clearly warn us about losing sight of our true purpose here on earth and getting caught up in vain arguments:

> Beware lest any man spoil you through philosophy and vain deceit, after the tradition of men, after the rudiments of the world, and not after Christ (Col. 2:8).

> O Timothy, keep that which is committed to thy trust, avoiding profane and vain babblings,

and oppositions of science falsely so called (1 Tim. 6:20).

As Christians, we should look for productive opportunities to share this information, but not to engage in vain arguments about it. Perhaps the best opportunities would be in the form of witnessing tools. Millions of people are worrying about their future. This is one opportunity that can be used to present a clear gospel and dispel their fears. Apologetics, creation sciences, and this information on global warming can all be used as witnessing tools for those who have been browbeaten and deceived by the evil one. They all offer hope (Heb. 11:1) for people's future.

Trusting His Word

> *But the day of the Lord will come as a thief in the night; in the which the heavens shall pass away with a great noise, and the elements shall melt with fervent heat, the earth also and the works that are therein shall be burned up* (2 Pet. 3:10).

Yes, the earth will ultimately be destroyed by global warming, but it will not be a *gradual* warming. The warming will occur *very* rapidly — in a single day. This text has attempted to present both scientific and biblical perspectives on the world as it deals with the 21st century. The last weather and environmental prediction that was 100 percent accurate was given at the time of Noah. It is fitting that we return to the biblical forecast to deal with these coming days. God has created this world and has plans for it in the present and the future. No amount of media or political hype can undermine the Word of God or alter our Creator's plan. It is your personal responsibility to avoid being distracted so that you can have an effective testimony to the gospel of Christ. Remember our opening story:

> With that, the very large warrior raised his spear — a mighty spear. The head alone weighed 15 pounds! The rays of the sun glistened on the sharpened edge of the

spear, which caused the small young man to smile as he exclaimed with all confidence, "Thou comest to me with a sword, and with a spear, and with a shield: but I come to thee in the name of the LORD of hosts, the God of the armies of Israel, whom thou hast defied. This day will the LORD deliver thee into mine hand; and I will smite thee, and take thine head from thee; and I will give the carcases of the host of the Philistines this day unto the fowls of the air, and to the wild beasts of the earth; that all the earth may know that there is a God in Israel. And all this assembly shall know that the LORD saveth not with sword and spear: for the battle is the LORD's, and he will give you into our hands" (1 Sam. 17: 45–47). With that, the small young man slung the stone at the very large warrior, and the rest is history.

Those who put their trust in Him should never fear the future nor ruin our system by trying to cope with this media hype about global warming. It is sad and ironic that more people seem to fear this gradual so-called global warming that is too slight to even be discerned by the human skin than the rapid blazing heat that will instantly engulf them at death if they do not turn to our Lord and Savior Jesus Christ. The first is grossly exaggerated media hype, while the second is a stern warning from our Creator Himself. Suppose that all the global-warming media hype is 100 percent true. Better yet, suppose global warming is really ten times worse than predicted. That heat would still be nothing compared to the heat that will be experienced by the unbelievers at the instant of their death. You have undoubtedly heard of people who have died a rapid fiery death. It is very disturbing to hear people say, "Well, at least it was quick." That is true if they were saved. But if they were not saved, had not given their hearts to Christ Jesus who gave His life for us, the heat of that earthly fire was only a brief precursor of the heat to come. Have you surrendered your heart and life to Christ? It is His desire that we should all live forever with Him! (2 Pet. 3:9.)

Appendix 1

Interesting Notes on the Calendar We Use Today

The calendar that the Western world currently uses tells us we have entered the year A.D. 2009. This calendar is based on a solar year, and the A.D. stands for anno domini (year of the Lord), which is related to the birth of Christ. Dionysius Exiguus, a Scythian monk (A.D. 525), determined that Christ was born at a date he set as A.D. 1, which was 754 years after the founding of Rome. The year and day of Christ's birth was also reported to be the 25th of Kislev (a month in the Jewish calendar which corresponds to December in the Julian and later Gregorian calendar) by Hippolytus (A.D. 165–235). Chrysostom (A.D. 345–407) wrote that December 25 was the correct date, and an early church document of A.D. 330 stated that it was 33 years exactly to the day from the immaculate conception to the crucifixion. With the crucifixion coming on Passover, as all Scripture teaches, this puts the conception just nine months before December 25, and all dates begin to fit into place. More recent research into the astronomical events surrounding Christ's birth and a better understanding of Josephus's statement concerning Herod's death and the lunar eclipse before Passover have shown Christ's birth date to be 1 B.C. Ernest L. Martin, director of the Foundation for Biblical Research in Pasadena, California, published this information in an article in *Christianity Today* entitled "The Celestial Pageantry Dating Christ's Birth."[1] Dionysius worked with the Julian calendar, which has since been replaced by the Gregorian calendar. The Gregorian calendar corrected an error in the Julian calendar's length of the year that caused an 11-day shift when the American colonies adopted it in 1752. This calendar is the one the Western world currently uses. An interesting aside here is that George Washington's birthday was listed in his mother's Bible as February 11, he being born before 1752, and afterward George celebrated it on the 22nd, or 11 days later.

---

1. Ernest L. Martin, "The Celestial Pageantry Dating Christ's Birth," *Christianity Today* (December 3, 1976), p. 17.

Appendix 2

Radiometric Dating

Extensive studies are being undertaken by the Institute for Creation Research (ICR) showing that, while carbon dating of living organisms is of some accuracy back to the time of the Flood, the dating of rocks by radiometric decay is absolutely worthless. Numerous rock samples were dated via independent laboratories and clearly indicated that the apparent age of a rock is consistently dependant on the isotopes being used to make the calculation. A single rock only has one "birth date." It cannot have different dates based on different measurement methods. Consequently, the time constants used to make these calculations cannot be constant. The extensive findings of these studies were presented at the fifth International Conference on Creationism held in the Pittsburgh area in August of 2003. The ICR group presented 19 peer-reviewed papers at the conference, and they were well received by the entire scientific community. One of the most significant results obtained in this research was the well-documented helium loss rate in the nuclear decay in zircons common in granitic rock. The helium loss rate is so high that almost all of it would have escaped if the uniformitarian age of the rocks of 1.5 billion years were true. But the crystals in granitic rock contain a very large amount of helium, supporting an age of only 6,000 years. In short, radiometric studies do not show an old earth.

Photo Credits

UPDATED & EXPANDED

INCLUDES A
FREE POWER
POINT CD

THE
YOUNG EARTH

The Real History of the Earth — Past, Present, and Future

REVISED
AND
EXPANDED

John Morris

POWERPOINT

CD

Includes FREE PowerPoint CD

8.5 x 11 • 144 pages • Casebound
Full-color interior • $17.99
ISBN 13: 978-0-89051-498-6

*This classic work from Dr. John Morris of the
Institute for Creation Research explodes popular
misconceptions about the age of the earth.
Morris studies the various creation theories,
geology, and culture to give a
true picture of Earth's history —
past, present, and future.*

Master
Books®
A Division of New Leaf Publishing Group
www.masterbooks.net